Modern Library Chronicles

KAREN ARMSTRONG on Islam
DAVID BERLINSKI on mathematics
RICHARD BESSEL on Nazi Germany
ALAN BRINKLEY on the Great Depression
IAN BURUMA on modern Japan
JAMES DAVIDSON on the Golden Age of Athens
SEAMUS DEANE on the Irish
FELIPE FERNÁNDEZ-ARMESTO on the Americas
LAWRENCE M. FRIEDMAN on law in America
JOHN LEWIS GADDIS on the Cold War
MARTIN GILBERT on the Long War, 1914–1945
PETER GREEN on the Hellenistic Age
JAN T. GROSS on the fall of Communism
ALISTAIR HORNE on the age of Napoleon
PAUL JOHNSON on the Renaissance
FRANK KERMODE on the age of Shakespeare
JOEL KOTKIN on the city
HANS KÜNG on the Catholic Church
BERNARD LEWIS on the Holy Land
FREDRIK LOGEVALL on the Vietnam War
MARK MAZOWER on the Balkans
JOHN MICKLETHWAIT and ADRIAN WOOLDRIDGE on the company
PANKAJ MISHRA on the rise of modern India
ANTHONY PAGDEN on peoples and empires
RICHARD PIPES on Communism
COLIN RENFREW on prehistory
JOHN RUSSELL on the museum
KEVIN STARR on California
ALEXANDER STILLE on fascist Italy
CATHARINE R. STIMPSON on the university
NORMAN STONE on World War I
MICHAEL STÜRMER on the German Empire
STEVEN WEINBERG on science
BERNARD WILLIAMS on freedom
A. N. WILSON on London
ROBERT S. WISTRICH on the Holocaust
GORDON S. WOOD on the American Revolution
JAMES WOOD on the novel

Also by Paul Fussell

Theory of Prosody in Eighteenth-Century England

Poetic Meter and Poetic Form

The Rhetorical World of Augustan Humanism: Ethics and Imagery from Swift to Burke

Samuel Johnson and the Life of Writing

The Great War and Modern Memory

Abroad: British Literary Traveling Between the Wars

The Boy Scout Handbook and Other Observations

Class: A Guide Through the American Status System

Thank God for the Atom Bomb and Other Essays

Wartime: Understanding and Behavior in the Second World War

BAD: or, the Dumbing of America

The Anti-Egotist: Kingsley Amis, Man of Letters

Doing Battle: The Making of a Skeptic

Uniforms: Why We Are What We Wear

Editor

English Augustan Poetry

The Ordeal of Alfred M. Hale

Siegfried Sassoon's Long Journey

The Norton Book of Travel

The Norton Book of Modern War

Coeditor

Eighteenth-Century English Literature

THE BOYS' CRUSADE

PAUL FUSSELL

THE BOYS' CRUSADE

The American Infantry in Northwestern Europe, 1944–1945

A MODERN LIBRARY CHRONICLES BOOK

THE MODERN LIBRARY

NEW YORK

 Published in the United States by Modern Library, an imprint of The Random House Publishing Group, a division of Random House, Inc., New York, and simultaneously in Canada by Random House of Canada Limited, Toronto.

Grateful acknowledgment is made to the following for permission to reprint previously published material:

ALGONQUIN BOOKS OF CHAPEL HILL AND ELLEN LEVINE LITERARY AGENCY/TRIDENT MEDIA GROUP: Excerpt from *The Medic: Life and Death in the Last Days of WWI* by Leo Litwak, copyright © 2001 by Leo Litwak. Rights throughout the British Commonwealth are controlled by the Ellen Levine Literary Agency/Trident Media Group. Reprinted by permission of Algonquin Books of Chapel Hill, a division of Workman Publishing, and the Ellen Levine Literary Agency/Trident Media Group.

ALFRED A. KNOPF, A DIVISION OF RANDOM HOUSE, INC.: Excerpt from *Before Their Time* by Robert Kotlowitz, copyright © 1997 by Robert Kotlowitz. Reprinted by permission of Alfred A. Knopf, a division of Random House, Inc.

LIBRARY OF CONGRESS CATALOGING-IN-PUBLICATION DATA
Fussell, Paul
The boys' crusade: the American infantry in northwestern Europe, 1944–1945 / Paul Fussell.—2003 Modern Library ed.
p. cm.—(Modern Library chronicles; 14)
"A Modern Library chronicles book."
Includes bibliographical references and index.
ISBN 0-679-64088-6
1. World War, 1939–1945—Campaigns—Western Front.
2. United States. Army—Infantry—History—20th century.
3. World War, 1939–1945—Regimental histories—United States.
I. Title. II. Series.

D756.3.F87 2003 940.54'214—dc21 2003044556

Modern Library website address: www.modernlibrary.com

Printed in the United States of America

2 4 6 8 9 7 5 3 1

To those on both sides
who suffered

Preface

Those intimate with the military and its ways have experienced the army's obsession with the Western European campaign of World War II. Even today, after all its subsequent action in the Middle Eastern deserts and the Asian swamps, the struggle in France and Germany in 1944 and 1945 seems to remain the army's point of reference for its conception of war—for the way it sees itself, its doctrine, its organization and training, its equipment, and its professional idioms. When the military looks for an instructive classic, it is the European war on the ground that is likely to be the model.

We may ask why, and this book may suggest a few answers. For one thing, unlike both the Korean and Vietnam wars, it ended well for the United States. And refracted in narrative, the war in Europe can be shown to possess a vivid moral structure, gratifying to both the historian and the normal patriotic reader.

At the ARCADIA Conference held in Washington in January 1942, Roosevelt and Churchill discussed what they should do to turn a losing war into a winning one. A subordinate attendant at the conference, a mere major general named Eisenhower, listened carefully and arrived at a depressing truth for the United States. He wrote in his diary, "We've got to go to Europe and fight." That is, air power alone, as some had been arguing, could not win the war, nor could a naval blockade nor other techniques less nasty than personal soldierly encounters on the ground. Infantry, he realized, would have to bear the ultimate burden, and winning the war by that means would be inescapably bloody.

Going to Europe and fighting there meant a dramatic increase in the small number of peacetime ground troops, and soon all over America training camps appeared: two-story white clapboard barracks, together with leveled-off parade grounds and firing ranges for small arms and artillery. And all had to be so superficial and temporary that after the war, the whole setup could be removed, leaving not a trace behind.

It was at scores of these camps that the draftees required by the ground forces were prepared for war. After a maximum of seventeen weeks' basic training—some received less—over two million young men were organized into eighty-nine divisions, each containing about twelve thousand soldiers. Not all fought, but the majority of these were shipped to the Continent to begin the process of destroying the German army, generally regarded as the best and the largest in the world. As Eisenhower conceived, winning the war would require "first, slugging with air at West Europe, to be followed by land attack as soon as possible." "Slugging with air": as a check on self-righteousness, it's well to remember that in July and August of 1943, the RAF and the U.S. Eighth Air Force burned to death thirty thousand civilians, of both genders and all ages, in Hamburg.

Actually, the United States had been surreptitiously in the war before the Japanese attack on Pearl Harbor and the German declaration of war that followed. The United States had been flagrantly violating its announced neutrality by sending Britain food, arms, tanks, aircraft, and ammunition, all at risk of being sunk by German U-boats, which prowled the Atlantic Coast looking for freighters. Sinkings were sometimes near enough to be watched by vacationers in Florida.

Once officially in the war, the American ground forces were prepared in England to obey the orders of the Combined Allied Chiefs of Staff. Addressing Eisenhower, the newly appointed Allied Supreme Commander, they said, "You will enter the Continent of Europe and . . . undertake operations aimed at the heart of Germany and the destruction of her armed forces."

On June 6, 1944, the slaughter of the frontal assault at Omaha Beach would warn of ample horrors to come. Until May 1945, the boys of America, with British and Canadian assistance, edged close to the "heart" of the enemy by overcoming in a series of encounters the retreating enemy at his successive defense lines. Some were rivers, some fortified areas, some shrewdly flooded ground. Most featured the new menace of antipersonnel mines, whose removal by combat engineers delayed attacks frequently. All these defenses were held with what seemed diabolical determination by an enemy fighting, it believed, for civilization's whole future existence.

Once loosed from the Normandy beachhead and its surroundings, the Americans faced the sobering fact that the nearest German border was 350 miles away, every foot of which had to be cleared of German soldiers. Getting to Germany took three months, even though the Americans were able to inject many new divisions into their line after invading southern France near Marseille on August 15. By August 25 German-occupied Paris was in sight and yielded without a struggle, and by December 15, the Americans were arrayed along the west bank of the Rhine from Holland to Switzerland, preparing for the final assault on Germany proper and the total destruction of its power to resist. Throughout these attacks in the west, the Americans coordinated their tactics with the Russian advance against Germany's eastern front. But by the fall of 1944, it became apparent that the Allies had seriously outrun their supplies, and as the weather worsened, they halted in eastern France and gradually despaired of ending the war before spring 1945. The war had four more months to run until the German surrender on May 8. Before the end of the carnage, 135,000 American boys were dead, 586,628 wounded.

The problem of offering an account of one dimension of the European war was how to squeeze eleven months of fighting and fear into a short book. Certainly not by trying to tell all, moving day by day from the Normandy landings (already sufficiently depicted in film and memoir) all the way to the surrender.

Finally I decided that the essence of the war on the ground might be conveyed by rigorous selection and intense focus on instructive contrasts and surprises—the fun of drinking and sex in London making up for the miseries of the troopship, and the shock of combat worse than any boy could have imagined.

It has been said that those who have not fought the Germans don't know what war is. In the Second World War, German troops, although gradually losing the war, were a hardened bunch compared with the boy members of what James Jones accurately called "a reluctant draftee army."

Now, almost sixty years after the horror, there has been a return, especially in popular culture, to military romanticism, which, if not implying that war is really good for you, does suggest that it contains desirable elements—pride, companionship, and the consciousness of virtue enforced by deadly weapons. In this book I have occasionally tried to confront this view with realistic details. Some readers may think my accounts of close warfare unjustifiably pessimistic in implication, but attention to the universal ironic gap between battle plans and battle actualities will suggest the ubiquity of much of my joyless material. There is nothing in infantry warfare to raise the spirits at all, and anyone who imagines a military "victory" gratifying is mistaken.

To get a feeling for the infantry war in Europe, one must take into account certain anomalies that seem to make no sense and cast a mantle of the absurd over bellicose events. (An example is what I will emphasize about the medical treatment of enemy prisoners.) Thus, while exploiting their technological sophistication by sending up rocket-propelled flying bombs and stratospheric ordnance to damage London and Antwerp, in the field the Germans relied on horses to drag around artillery pieces, kitchens, and similar heavy loads, as if replaying the techniques of the Napoleonic Wars. In a war heralded as an up-to-date affair of motor vehicles and rapid mobility, the infantry of both sides walked more often than they were conveyed to their duty by trucks. To be sure, there were tanks and half-tracks and jeeps, but much of the fighting took place without heavy equipment at all, the infantry performing its role with rifles, hand grenades, machine guns, and mortars and using tactics unchanged since the First World War and even the Civil War. "Marching fire," General Patton's favorite mode of infantry attack (firing at the enemy from the hip while walking toward him), combined simultaneous fire and movement in a way useful since the Indian pacifications of the nineteenth century.

And perhaps this is the place to remind readers of the meaning of a few terms. A *squad* consisted of twelve men armed with rifles and led by a sergeant. One of the men carried a heavy BAR, a Browning Automatic Rifle, a relic of the First World War, and no match for the modern German automatic weapons. A *platoon* consisted of three such squads led by a lieutenant, and a *company*, four platoons, one with heavy weapons like mortars and water-cooled machine guns, led by a captain. Formed up for an attack, one can imagine all of them scared to death.

It may be necessary for war to employ adolescent boys, but that's no reason to assume them as readers of military history. The historiography I've been drawn to abjures attractive cuteisms like "the Big Red One," "Hell on Wheels," and "the Rainbow Division," as well as charming, troop-friendly allusions to things like "the deuce-and-a-half truck." The world of ground warfare can never be truly recalled by such stuff, which belongs to the history of sentimental show business, not the history of real human action and emotion, especially as triggered by intimate horror, death, and sorrow. In my view, a chronicle should deal with nothing but the truth and thus serve as a small warning for the future.

And it is worth suggesting that for some of the boy survivors, now aged around eighty, the end of the war was equivalent in many ways to the end of Europe and of European pretenses to superiority. It remained a place perhaps to travel to, but it was now stained so deeply by folly and cruelty that it could no longer justify the reverence Henry

James and others once lavished on it as an immutable guide to manners and intellectual technique.

Historian Modris Eksteins quotes an educated German woman's conclusions about the war:

> One can only regard our present situation as the quintessence of irony in the whole history of the world. . . . We will never get over this bloody calvary. We have grown old and weary to death. One sits and searches one's brain for an explanation. . . . What was the point of it all, what rhyme or reason was there for this desperate, ruinous destruction? Was it just a satanic game?

The elderly American Boy Crusaders have now a few years left to ponder Eksteins's feelings:

> "Even if surrounded with explanations," Gunter Grass has written, "Auschwitz can never be grasped." The same is true of the murderous military strategies of the two world wars, of Stalin's homicidal policies, and of the fire-bombing of civilians in undefended cities. Nineteen forty-five marked the nadir of Western Civilization.

And the Boy Crusaders were there to watch the whole dismal performance.

Acknowledgments

For their interest and help, I want to thank Michael Barber, Harriette Behringer, Clifford J. Case, Thomas Childers, Sam Fussell, Toby Harke, Robert Kotlowitz, Scott Moyers, Seth Notes, Tim O'Brien, Mercedes Ruiz, J. T. Scanlan, Roger Spiller, Studs Terkel, and Russell Weigley.

Weigley is the historian I have relied on with the greatest appreciation for the accuracy of his scholarship and his sensitivity to humane values. Others in this category are Martin Blumenson and Charles MacDonald.

There is a lot of Robert Kotlowitz in this book. He is a person I admire for his immunity to the degradations of infantry combat and for his humor and his sympathy for his fellow soldiers, even when they're behaving badly.

Gwen Gatto has again rendered herself indispensable by her cheerful command of the word processor. I thank her most warmly for her sharp eye and her patience.

Contents

THE BOYS' CRUSADE

THE BOY CRUSADERS

When Ike Eisenhower was a boy, European history was more avidly pursued in schools than now, and it's also possible that he knew a bit about the Crusades from his own reading, if he hadn't heard about them in church—his family was pious—or at elementary or high school or even at West Point. In any event, the imagery of the Crusades was lodged strongly in his mind. In an Order of the Day given or read to "Soldiers, Sailors, and Airmen of the Allied Expeditionary Force," just before the invasion of Normandy, he informed them: "You are about to embark upon the Great Crusade, toward which we have striven these many months." And, once successfully over, he would title his memoir of the war *Crusade in Europe.*

Eisenhower was not the only one conscious during the war of the Crusades. One of the enemy, Panzer leader Hans von Luck, had occasion three times to recall a poem about a military moment in the Crusades whose horrors resembled those he witnessed in the Falaise Pocket in 1944. He writes, " 'Man, horse, and truck, by the Lord were struck.' This saying, from a poem on the battles of the Crusaders in Palestine about 1213, had come to my mind twice before: in December, 1941, by Moscow, and in 1943 in North Africa."

The date 1213 suggests the so-called Children's Crusade, about whose actuality some historians have doubts. In the year 1212, it is said, an odd army set out from France and Germany. Its purpose was to liberate the Holy Land from the profane grip of Islam. This Crusade is reputed to have numbered fifty thousand young people, of whom only three thousand survived the attentions of pirates, slave dealers, and brothel keepers. Whether actual or mythical, the Children's Crusade can't help suggesting many dimensions of American youth's curious, violent journey eastward over France and Germany in the Second World War. Kurt Vonnegut invokes *The Children's Crusade* as a sardonic alternative title for his novel *Slaughterhouse Five,* which measures many significant features of that war and those "children."

I intend no disrespect to the memory of Dwight D. Eisenhower by examining his term *crusade.* It made some sense at the moment, even if many of the still unblooded troops were likely to ridicule it. If they read or heard the Supreme Commander's words at all, they were doubtless embarrassed to have so highfalutin a term applied to their forthcoming performances and their feelings about them. It is likely that many never saw the sheet of paper on which the word appeared, and if the message was read to them (in the wind and the rain), their military experience so far had inclined them to greet all official utterances with scorn and skepticism. Indeed, when such pronouncements were read aloud they often ridiculed them noisily, until silenced by a sergeant's "At ease!"

At this distance, it may not be easy to remember that the European ground war in the west was largely fought by American boys seventeen, eighteen, and nineteen years old. At seventeen you could enlist if you had your parents' written permission, but most boys waited until they were drafted at age eighteen. (Actually, the army contained numerous illicit seventeen-year-olds, their presence as soldiers more or less regularized by false papers not rigorously inquired into.) Some of these men-children shaved but many did not need to. Robert Kotlowitz remembers bayonet drill. "We aimed, thrust, slashed or whichever—screaming 'Kill! Kill!' in our teen-age voices." Not a few soldiers hopeful of food packages from home specified Animal Crackers, which, one soldier said, "can do wonders for low morale." (Perhaps what troops were recalling when seeking this specialty was eight-year-old Shirley Temple singing "Animal Crackers in My Soup.") At the same time, the infantrymen, not yet versed in the adult conventions of the high-class uses of wine, did not wait until after dinner to sip a little cognac. In quantity, it often replaced water in their canteens.

Who were these boys, who bitched freely but seldom cried, even when wounded? What did they have in common? Most had sufficient emotional control not to express angry envy of those (like, say, nonflying air corps troops) who had a nicer, safer war.

These infantry soldiers, if they weren't children, weren't quite men either, even if officers commonly addressed groups of them as such. One medical aidman was typical in referring to his patients as boys. Explaining in a letter home the workings of the casualty-clearing system, he falls naturally into phrases like these—a boy gets hurt; the injured boy; leaves space for another boy; the wounded boy; as each boy comes in; a brief history of the boy and his diagnosis—the last of which refers to the official tag fastened to the soldier's jacket or, as our aidman puts it, to "the boy's coat." Wounded officers passing through the aid station were never called boys, although many were almost as young.

Taken as a whole, the boys had a powerful propulsion of optimism, a sense that the war couldn't last forever, and that if anyone was going to get wounded, it would not be them. They had a common ability to simulate courage despite actuality: that is, a certain amount of dramatic talent, plus a vivid appreciation of black humor, involving plenty of irony. They had sufficient physical stamina to survive zero-degree cold from time to time, and considerable elementary camping skills of the sort common among civilian fishermen and hunters, which lots of survivors became after the war. They had to have fine eyesight, good enough to detect planted antipersonnel mines by their little triggers of thin wire protruding aboveground. They had to have a pack rat's skill in collecting small objects, like looted knives and forks. And preeminently, they had to have extraordinary luck. One infantryman's mother exhorted him to be careful. He answered: "You can't be careful. You can only be lucky."

And these young troops got along with one another because they usually shared certain beliefs:

1. America is the best country in the world because it is the only really modern one.
2. It is the world leader in technology, producing the bulk of the good cars, and, in unbelievably large quantities, airplanes and tanks, which, being the best in the world, are going to win the war. They are certainly better than anything the Germans and the Japs can make. (Only the brightest and boldest of the troops perceived that American tanks were seriously outgunned by German ones and, when struck by a shell, were likely to burst into flames, almost as a matter of course. This tendency earned them the name Ronsons, after the popular cigarette lighter.) Among the troops, only the finely tuned noted the superiority of the German machine guns. Discovery of these facts was demoralizing, and a problem confronting the brighter U.S. in-

fantrymen was rationalizing away these sorry truths when among dumber people.

3. The American army, despite its screwups, is the best ever in providing the troops with clothing, food, lodging, personal weapons, and security.

These credulous youths were the products of American high schools, and differences of race, religion, and social class did not significantly alter their adherence to this code of belief or influence their common hatreds, which can be specified as follows:

1. Officers of any kind, especially those not to a degree redeemed by sharing troops' hardships, and those pursuing in wartime their peacetime professions in uniform, like medicine, optometry, or medical administration. These phonies were granted officer rank and beautiful dress uniforms without having to undergo the usual price of painful infantry training.
2. The French, and quite justly too: they spoke a language impossible to learn and embarrassing to pronounce, and worse, they required the help of strangers (especially Americans) to win their wars, both the First World War and this one. In his most famous harangue of the troops, General Patton had enunciated the American view of people who lose wars or battles: "Americans love a winner. Americans will not tolerate a loser." And the French of all types were distinctly snotty toward their saviors.
3. Stay-at-homes exempt from the war by virtue of largely invisible ailments, like punctured eardrums, high blood pressure, flat feet, or a "nervous condition." Even self-proclaimed "homosexuality."
4. Anyone occupying in combat a position to the rear of the infantryman. Included are soldiers in the artillery, all engineers except combat engineers, and certainly the various

> staff, afraid to visit the line and to see what's actually happening there.

Military historian Roger Spiller, who has spent decades studying the embarrassing actualities of battle, quotes with approval Bernard Knox, who writes, "It is true of every war that much as he may fear and perhaps even hate the enemy opposing him, the combat infantryman broods with deep and bitter resentment over the enormous number of people in his rear who sleep safely at night." And it was an enormous number. Spiller explains: "Of the millions of Americans sent overseas by the Army during World War II, only 14 percent were infantrymen. Those 14 percent took more than 70 percent of all the battle casualties among overseas troops." As Captain Harold P. Leinbaugh, author of the memoir *The Men of Company K,* proclaims, "We were the Willie Lomans of the war." Or, as some coarser speakers have put it, "the niggers." Soldiers who fought in North Africa and Southern Italy, struck by the squalor and filth of the peasants, thought of them as "the Infantry of the World."

"Adolescent fervor" is Robert Kotlowitz's term for those characteristics of male youth that can be honed and intensified by military training. "The Army understood that fervor and used it," he writes. "All armies do; they depend upon it." Adolescent fervor in the form it assumed before bullets and artillery and mines ruined it is pleasantly registered by Edward W. Wood Jr., an enthusiastic—no, ecstatic—soldier as he participated in the victorious pursuit of the enemy in late August 1944:

> To be nineteen years old, to be nineteen and an infantryman, to be nineteen and fight for the liberation of France from the

Nazis in the summer of 1944! That time of hot and cloudless blue days when the honeybees buzzed about our heads and we shouted strange phrases in words we did not understand to men and women who cheered us as if we were gods. That summer, that strangely glorious summer, when we rushed across France, the Nazis fleeing just ahead of us. *Drive east, drive east.* South of Paris the day it was liberated, across the Marne to Château-Thierry (battlefields of the war in which my father and uncle had fought), then Reims with its cathedral, the most beautiful structure I had ever seen in my life, its magical flying buttresses brilliant against the August sky. Each village we entered started another party for us, as we shared bottles of wine hoarded since 1940 and kisses from wet-mustached men and smooth-cheeked women while we hurled cigarettes and chocolates from our armored half-track and got drunk together and laughed and cried and screamed, for we had freed them from evil. For that glorious moment, the dream of freedom lived and we were ten feet tall.

A few weeks later, "in action" with his unit, he is ill-treated by a German artillery shell, which tears away his buttocks. In his book *On Being Wounded* he recalls it all, and a ghastly story of suffering and shame it is.

In May 1945, infantryman Mitchell Sharpe writes his mother, who has told him of the death in combat of his friend Neal:

DEAR MOM:

I couldn't possibly feel any worse if you had written one of the immediate family had died. I keep thinking of him like that kid . . . lying off the path as if he were asleep. I see him lying on his back, arms overhead, with eyes and mouth open, as if asking, "God, why?" If you could only see us kids killed at eighteen, nineteen, and twenty, fighting in a country that

> means nothing to us. . . . Kids that have never had a crack at life. Some have never worked and earned money and felt proud, . . . never felt the temporary exhilaration of being drunk, never slept with a girl.

Mitchell Sharpe closes his letter by visualizing "the thousands of Neals buried from Normandy to Munich."

First Time Abroad

For American troops, the first unpleasant act in their active and dangerous participation in what has been misleadingly termed the Good War was throwing up in the transports conveying them to the United Kingdom. Most threw up only for the first several hours, but some never stopped for the seven days or more of the journey. Another cause of unhappiness was the augmentation of their normal hatred of officers. While the men ate terrible food twice a day standing up, the officers, in an elegant restaurant several decks above, sat down to white table linen, nice cutlery, friendly service by stewards, and infinitely better food, hardly different from the cuisine rich transatlantic passengers had enjoyed before the war.

For most men, and officers as well, this was their maiden voyage, and when they arrived in Liverpool, they began to experience the foreign for the first time. They had been primed by Eric Knight's booklet *A Short Guide to Great Britain.* (For their part, the locals were gently prepared for surprises by Louis MacNeice's *Meet the U.S. Army.*)

There was no doubt that despite the vague similarity of the two idioms, Britain was a world away from the environment the boy Yanks knew and loved. For one thing, cars were tiny and drove on the wrong side of the road. Victuals were vastly different: the food was cottony and bland, the beer soft and lukewarm. When after a lot of disgusting beer a boy sought a place to urinate, he found the fixtures laughably archaic. Bathtubs were not overly common, showers virtually nonexistent. It seemed to rain all the time, and there was little central heating, only tiny gas stoves that hardly worked. Everything seemed called by a different name: a drugstore (which sold only drugs) was called a chemist's, and condoms tended to be sold by hairdressers, i.e., barbers. The coinage was irrational and required constant study if one were to avoid being cheated. The five-pound bill (British, *note*) looked like a diploma. The language was replete with pitfalls. You had to steer clear of *bum,* for example, and *bloody,* and instead of *excuse me,* you had to say *soddy.* Compounding these oddities, British speech, in addition to its strange pronunciation, was fond of understatement and straight-faced irony, both seldom practiced in the United States.

Almost two and a half years passed between the arrival of the first American troops and their nervous, serious departure for Normandy. Although their main business in the United Kingdom was training and toughening, their recreation (drinking aside) was largely women, both innocents and prostitutes. And for British women, the Yanks were nothing short of a gift.

First of all, their hygiene was better than that of their local counterparts, who smelled of underarm sweat, especially when dancing. The Yanks had recourse to something new, little jars of Arrid and Odorono, not to mention shaving lotion. The women also loved the American uniform jacket, with classy lapels like the RAF's. If the American soldier dolled up for a date looked like a gentleman, the British soldier, with his coarse wool battle-dress jacket with working-class collar, looked like a slob. Instead of the British soldiers' noisy hobnailed boot soles, the GIs had nice, silent rubber ones. But the Yanks' biggest appeal for the British female was their comparative riches, which, among many other features, gave credence to the joke, "Have you heard about the new utility knickers [U.S., *panties*]? One Yank and they're off."

Given all this, it is not hard to understand the British troops' bitter hostility toward the GIs, not to mention the outrage caused by their vastly different pay scales. Expressed in U.S. dollars, a British private was paid $2.82 a week; an American private, $13.84. A British second lieutenant earned $67.42 a month; an American, $162.50. The effect of this upon "dating" need not be emphasized, nor its contribution to the obvious bad blood between British and American forces, who sedulously avoided each other's company. The whole American air of excess and even luxury can be illustrated by the assumed toilet-paper needs of the two armies. The American army estimated that one of its soldiers would use 22.5 sheets per day. The British estimate for its troops was three sheets.

Sensing increasingly as the weeks went by what they were going to face on the beaches of France, the GIs did not stint on sexual enjoyment, and London was the favorite place for it. Well supplied with army-issue condoms, you met your woman on the sidewalk and began by asking, in the blackout, "Got a light?" The match flame would tell you if she was too old, ugly, or dirty to be sexworthy. That ascertained satisfactorily, you took her to Hyde Park, Green Park, or Kensington Gardens, or if that was too far, you had her standing up against a wall. Countless British girls were deceived by the folk rumor that you couldn't get pregnant if you did it standing up against a building. GI Louis Simpson remembers sidewalk sounds: "Come on, Yank. Ahnly two quid!" and he adds, "Henry James, had he heard the obscenities issuing from an air-raid shelter, might have revised in some degree his comparisons of American coarseness and English refinement."

Heavy work was required by both American and British public relations personnel for concealing the discomfort with and often severe dislike of each army for the other. The Americans, especially those on the staff, found the British supercilious and stuffy, constantly patronizing their ally by claiming greater military experience, earned in the many months before the tardy, unwilling Americans were forced into action by Pearl Harbor after their apparent satisfaction with the defeat of France and Britain in 1940. And when they considered more distant history, the British found themselves still annoyed by the independence of the United States in the first place and its impudent departure from the Empire, as well as the embarrassing example it set of republican freedom for restive colonies like India. The British were also understandably annoyed by America's being untouched by the bombings, blackouts, and rationing they had endured, and seeming often unimaginative and unsympathetic about Britain's relative poverty and obsolescence.

When the boy John Keegan saw hordes of American troops taking over the countryside, he assumed that the American presence in Britain meant that the Yanks were generously putting themselves under British command. He finally made the humbling discovery that this was not the case at all and that the Americans would constitute the bulk of the means by which the war in the West could be won. Churchill helped illuminate his stubborn countrymen when, after the invasion of Sicily, he reminded the Commons: "Since 1776 we have not been in the position of being able to decide the policy of the United States." From then on, it was clear to all, if unacceptable to most, that Britain would not be controlling either political or military events. No wonder they felt humiliated and undone, especially because the Yanks were so ignorant and vulgar. No wonder ill feelings arose both in the British army and on the home front. In the army, British weapons and equipment were visibly inferior to the Americans': the flat British helmet clearly offered less protection; compared with the eight-round semiautomatic rifle of the GIs, the British Enfield was bolt-operated and slow; the British troops had one uniform only, for both fighting and "walking out"; and they even had limited dental care, primarily emphasizing extraction.

The news spread rapidly to civilians that U.S. privates appeared better dressed than British officers and that the Americans were "so much better off than our boys." Even those who did not date them couldn't help noticing that "they smelled so nice." When objectors to the Yanks' presence and rowdy behavior complained that they were "overpaid, oversexed, and over here," the Americans, who may have sensed a more authentic reason for British annoyance, answered that British troops were "underpaid, undersexed, and under Eisenhower."

The last fact occasioned much bitterness, some justified, among senior British officers. Because many more American than British troops would fight and be killed, an American would have to hold the office of Supreme Commander. But British officers couldn't help noticing that Eisenhower had never commanded combat troops: his distinction was that of a staff officer only. His main critic was General (later Field Marshal) Sir Bernard Law Montgomery, who was pleased to draw attention to the disparity between his battle command experience and the Supreme

Commander's. Monty had led combat troops in World War I and been decorated for bravery. As a lieutenant, he had been shot in the lung, and his courage brought him promotion to captain. He more than once said that while Ike had never commanded troops in battle, "I've commanded everything there is to command. I never missed a single position: platoon, company, battalion, brigade, division, army corps, army, group of armies. That's rare. That's the way to do it."

Monty annoyed his allies mightily by seldom curbing such quarrelsome self-praise. Some sort of psychological uncertainty was his trouble and he needed to be praised at all times. This state of mind might be seen as a midget version of the United Kingdom's postcolonial shock. After all, one of the world's great empires was being brought to its knees, and worse, by a group from one of its former possessions. A group, almost, of "natives." Monty found it hard to be minimally polite to Americans, even to Eisenhower, his superior officer. Once, Monty's attitude of pedant and scold so annoyed the Supreme Commander that Ike was moved to say, "Steady, Monty! You can't talk to me like that. I'm your boss." The friction between the two became so well known that the troops of both sides found it easy to believe that they had had a fistfight in the presence of troops over the disasters of Monty's OPERATION MARKET GARDEN. One American complaint about Monty's generalship was that he was too cautious, too unwilling to take risks. But his apparent disinclination to accept necessary casualties arose from his knowledge that unlike the States, Britain was running out of men: he could foresee a moment when there would be no more replacements for his army. Still, it is amazing that the egotism and arrogance of one mere man could occasion so much trouble.

Another cause of friction between these two allies was American racial policy. The Americans' desire to follow stateside rules about the segregation of blacks from whites gave great offense in Britain and caused no end of trouble. In Britain the "problem" was unknown. But many American officers and men came from the Southern states; they expected strict segregation abroad, and in the United Kingdom they refused to use facilities open to black and white alike. There was loud British objection to this unlawful and distasteful social segregation. Race riots broke out, and the city of Bristol was the scene of one of the worst. Under American pressure, the city had become divided into two recreational areas, with no black-white mixing allowed, but the black soldiers became convinced that they'd been assigned the least desirable pubs. One Saturday night, four hundred black and white GIs began fighting, requiring 120 MPs with truncheons to deal with the mess. Before order was restored, several men had been severely injured. One had been killed. In the nearby town of Cheltenham, the citizens grew violently angry at the white treatment of blacks and learned a new word when white officers termed them "nigger lovers." Fights broke out when white GIs saw girls going out with blacks—most girls found the blacks more polite and decent than the whites. Indeed, British civilians seemed almost unanimous in finding the black GI an improvement over the white. One wit said, "I don't mind the Yanks but I can't say I care for those white chaps they've brought with them." George Orwell found that "the only American soldiers with decent manners are the Negroes," and a woman serving at a troop canteen said, "We find the colored troops are much nicer to deal with. We like serving them, they're always so courteous and have a very natural charm that most of the white miss. Candidly,

I'd far rather serve a regiment of the dusky lads than a couple of whites."

Even after the GIs left, racial problems remained. "There were scenes of anguish in August, 1945," reported the *Bristol Sunday Pictorial*, "as hundreds of screaming girls besieged the barracks where the black soldiers were packing up. They broke down barriers, and at the rail station, it is said, they shouted, 'To hell with the US color bar. We want our colored sweethearts.' "

But in the spring of 1944, as the sudden massive move of the Yanks and their vehicles alerted watchers to the imminence of the bloody work they were brought over for, some of the customary friction dropped away and some of the jokes seemed to need revision:

> YANK: "I've come from Fort Bragg."
> BRITON: "Yes, I can believe that."

Says one Yank: "It was no longer them and us." Despite general relief that the Americans were gone, there was now an unavoidable understanding of what these alien boys were there for and what was going to happen to a great many of them. One American, Bob Sheehan, recalls the soldier's view: "Ahead lay a dangerous trip into the unknown. There was an element of potential disaster about the whole enterprise. We mostly felt that we would win in the end, but this attack *could* fail and then another start would have to be made. It was the kind of thinking that made many cigarettes glow in the darkness when we should have been all asleep." It might now be sensed that the drunkenness and the whoring were largely a distraction and relief from troubling, unmentionable thoughts.

—

What did these American soldiers look like as they left behind the comforts of Britain and set off on "the Great Crusade"? The United States Army, or at least its soldiers, goes in for a widespread habit of uniform usage best designated *sloppery.* This look was noted by most Europeans witnessing American soldiers in the Second World War, astonished by their apparent sloppiness in contrast with Continental military norms. Victor Klemperer, a German civilian, writes of his first sight of U.S. armored troops: "They are not soldiers in the Prussian sense at all. They do not wear uniforms at all but overalls, . . . combinations of high trousers and blouse, all in gray-green. . . . The steel helmet is worn as comfortably as a hat, pushed forward or back, as it suits them." The boy Keegan was enraptured by the sloppery of the GIs he saw in the countryside before the invasion—leaning against buildings, always adopting comfortable instead of military postures, driving their jeeps with one leg outside, foot on the fender, and when possible ostentatiously steering with one hand. Ernie Pyle saw U.S. soldiers as unique because "we admittedly are not a rigid-minded people. . . . Our boys sing in the streets, unbutton their shirt collars, laugh and shout and forget to salute." (*Forget* is probably too kind; *refuse* would be more accurate.) To suggest all this, one could probably invoke terms like Huck Finnery, or the Conscript's Revenge. Conscious sloppery is a way of saying, "I'm not really a powerless part of an institution so unfair, stupid, and silly as the army. I'm still the careless boy from Winnetka that I used to be, and I'm determined forever to be my own boss. Screw you all."

To understand these boys, one should know a little about what they wore and carried. Because the U.S. Army (or the Army of the United States, to distinguish the conscript army from the proud, professional one) was a dynamic and always changing one, the moment it is examined, it is in the process of change. At first, the troops landing in, say, North Africa wore old-fashioned canvas lace-up leggings (pronounced *leggins*) and high leather shoes. But soon more up-to-date footwear became official: boots made from high shoes with a five-inch rough leather cuff added on top; and as the winter worsened, leather and rubber shoepacs, worn during the infamous trench-foot menace running from December 1944 to spring 1945. Tucked into the boots or shoepacs were wool trousers, the same as those normally part of the dress uniform, and once the layering principle against cold was mastered, the wool trousers were covered by another pair, of dark green two-ply tightly woven cotton. These matched the new field jacket with four outer pockets, each large enough to hold a cardboard box of K-rations. One ex-soldier reports that in December, it was so cold that "I was wearing a suit of summer underwear, two suits of heavy long wool underwear, two sets of wool pants, a wool shirt, a wool sweater, an old field jacket, a new combat jacket, two pairs of wool socks, combat boots, wool gloves, a wool knit cap, and a steel helmet."

As diarrhea began to afflict virtually all the frontline troops, the need to stay warm by maximum layering conflicted with the need to take things off rapidly. One man testifies: "I had on three suits of underwear and two pairs of pants and had to go quickly. This took some quick unbuttoning." There were of course myriads of painful accidents that did nothing to promote morale and self-respect. "One soldier, aiming for the latrine, slipped and fell in the mud and crapped in his clothes. He lay there and cried in frustration." That sort of hell was never publicized but constituted a constant, unavoidable part of infantry experience.

Around his waist, the rifleman wore a "web" cartridge

belt with pockets for the eight-round M-1 clips. The ammunition load could be increased by adding one or more cotton bandoleers, worn across the chest. Raincoats were folded and stuffed into the back of the cartridge belt. It also held a first-aid dressing and a canteen, officially filled with water but, this being France, not always innocent of wine. Hooked to the belt might also be an Infantryman's Friend, a combination pick and shovel for digging in.

Most soldiers carried an M-1 rifle but also had to carry pieces of mortars and machine guns. Boys who aspired to a superbellicose look wore a trench knife on the belt, together with the official bayonet in its scabbard. On the back of the helmet were often to be seen significant painted one-inch-wide stripes. A horizontal one designated a noncommissioned officer, a vertical one an officer. Both were rather misleading in implying that the wearer was out in front, "leading" the troops. Actually, in a proper attack, a platoon was preceded by two men called scouts, presumably skilled in observation and deduction, able to give early warning of the enemy's location. In theory, the commanding officer came next. But as the ground war in Europe wore on, so many lieutenants leading from the front were destroyed that their presence there was no longer insisted on or expected. Groups of men wearing naked helmets without dark green camouflage nets were obviously so new and pathetic as to be noticed, patronized, and set right.

There was one advantage in being in an attack, and only one: there, a soldier was seldom troubled by the chickenshit to be met with in the rear. At the real front there was no such thing as being "out of uniform," for the soldier looked like a tramp with individual variations all the time, and officers were indistinguishable from the lowest dogfaces. Neither wore anything like insignia, and to look as dirty as possible was socially meritorious. A lot has been said about the white camouflage outfits worn by the troops in the winter, but they were so scarce that most men wore mattress covers or tablecloths, bedsheets, or white towels stolen from nearby civilian premises.

The teenagers of the infantry, deprived of such customary status totems as the Model A Ford Roadster and in-vogue clothing, were forced to find new status symbols. Most depended on the seniority of a person or unit in the European Theater of Operations. Newcomers were regarded with a degree of not always silent contempt, and replacements were the most conspicuous newcomers. There were many signals by which new arrivals could be detected. Cleanliness was one of them. Soldiers or officers in new or neat clothing, not yet ripped in places or grease-stained all over from C- and K-rations, were easy to spot as targets of disdain. Company officers wearing gold or silver bars on shirt collars were clearly unacquainted yet with the veritable law of the line that unless officers' insignia were covered by a scarf, enemy snipers would pick them off first. (Probably quite false, but believed by all.) The helmet net could become a low-social-class giveaway by the absence of a worn-out portion at the top; when the helmet was taken off and placed upside down on the ground, the net should be worn away. In many infantry divisions, rumor held that if the chin strap of the helmet was fastened and worn in the correct way, the wearer ran the risk of being beheaded by a close explosion, which, it was said, would tear off helmet and head at once. This probably began as a practical joke, like sending a newcomer to get a left-handed screwdriver, but it was widely believed, and officers and men alike fastened the chin strap around the back of the helmet.

Units newly arrived on the line—especially the high-numbered infantry divisions that appeared in 1944—were held to lack class, and members of the 102nd, the 103rd, and the 104th Divisions felt the shame attaching to the ignorant and the out-of-place. Long-serving divisions earned similar scorn when finally their original men were carried off dead or wounded and replaced by raw, green ex-ASTP (Army Specialized Training Program) boys or angry ex–air corps personnel.

(Military history, as commonly practiced, often errs in its easy devotion to "order of battle," which means narrating mortal encounters by simply designating the units taking part. This might do if the units are the proud, largely static regiments of the British army, which do their own training, but in the American military, distinguished units very soon become undistinguished as they are inevitably diluted and enfeebled by the inclusion of not just relatively untrained but hyperscared replacements, and the original, proud spirit of the unit is handed unearned to pitiable youths angry to have been snatched into the infantry from the air corps or the ASTP. Until finally in the originally good divisions, hardly an original soldier is left, and the whole army is all of a piece, that is, second-rate. Near the end of the war, infantry divisions with sterling histories, like the 1st or the 4th or the 101st Airborne, become lamentable caricatures of what they once were and resemble nothing so much as the newest of the new divisions, populated by the inadequately trained and the largely unwilling.)

THE FORTITUDE SECRET

The boys destined to land on the beaches of Normandy would have felt less anxiety if they had known about a weapon kept secret until well after the war. This weapon did not involve explosives and shells, sharpened bayonets and thirty-caliber bullets, but knowledge—knowledge the Allies were not supposed to have. The knowledge was of top-secret German plans, orders, and records, and the Allies had been in possession of it since 1943.

Allied intelligence knew the Germans were aware that an invasion of France from England was being readied. But two things about it the Germans did not know: the place and the time. What should they defend and when should they defend it?

The secret operation was primarily British and it bore the code name FORTITUDE. The idea was to deceive the enemy into believing the invasion was going to take place somewhere it was not and thus lure enemy divisions and reserves away from the place where they would be useful. The Germans had to be persuaded that any Allied landing in, say, Normandy was really only a feint designed to conceal plans for the real invasion, two hundred miles north in the Pas de Calais. This could be made to seem credible because it involved the shortest distance to the assumed Allied target, Berlin. In aid of this deception, elaborate fraudulent army camps were built northwest of Dover, and they were presumably occupied by the immense strength of FUSAG—First United States Army Group. This unit was entirely fictitious, but its divisions were given credible identity and reality by constant radio traffic, exactly like that expected among real army units. Roads and trucks and tanks added to the verisimilitude, but the last two were made not of steel but inflated rubber. Rubber and papier-mâché landing craft were assembled and deliberately ill camouflaged in appropriate ports.

FUSAG was said to be commanded by General Patton, and he was actually seen tongue-wagging in the proper places from time to time, going about his duties as army group commander.

Sometimes cruel methods had to be used to strengthen the impression that the convenient Pas de Calais would be the target of the invasion. To move troops and reserves quickly to this fancied battlefield, Hitler would have to use railways, and to strengthen the idea that it was these railways that were dangerous to the Allied plan, lots of bombs were dropped on French railways, railway stations, and, alas, railway towns, where many French civilians were killed. Even the Germans found it hard to believe that their enemy would kill so many civilians merely to maintain a deception. To make the deception further credible, the Allies dropped more bombs and killed more French citizens around the Pas de Calais area than in Normandy. This was certainly unfortunate and cruel, but the whole war, Allied as well as German, was unfortunate and cruel, even if this aspect seems often forgotten.

The now famous XX (Doublecross) system also went into action to help win the war by any means, nice or nasty. All the spies that Germany had managed to insinuate into Britain with shortwave radios for transmitting their reports back to Hamburg were without exception captured by the British. Once in hand, they were "turned" and secretly joined the Allied cause. Now, each spy had an Allied "minder" (formerly "case officer") who told the German agent what to send and was careful to coordinate the reports with deceptions emanating from the whole FUSAG operation. As onetime intelligence colonel Nigel West has said recently, "Strategic deception is now recognized as an essential component of any major military undertaking, and without exception the textbooks agree that the ingenious scheme, code-named FORTITUDE, dreamed up to mislead the enemy over the long-expected invasion of Europe in 1944, was the most successful ever executed."

Unknown now, and probably unknown forever, are the methods used to persuade all the captured German agents in the United Kingdom to switch allegiance, but they doubtless included threats of blackmail and torture and recourse to the immediate firing squad, entirely appropriate in the case of captured spies.

In addition to the XX system, the Allies had another highly secret intelligence tool of inestimable value. This was code-named ULTRA. With Polish help, the British had obtained a sample German encoding machine named ENIGMA, designed to send and receive, with its typewriter keyboard, coded messages. The Germans thought the system was entirely safe and unbreakable, but after intense cryptographic study, the British mastered its workings. They now had secret access to German field orders, messages, plans, and other crucial matter revealing identification of military units, troop strengths, disposition of units, troop movements, and even tactics. The American troops knew nothing about this, and indeed, no one in the Allied armies knew about it but a few officers at the very top.

General Montgomery, like all Allied commanders of armies, had constant access to the news from ULTRA, and many now believe that in news conferences, where his egotism and self-promotion gave offense, he may have exaggerated that pose consciously in order not to risk betraying the secret of ULTRA, which had made his decisions less original and risky than they had seemed at the time.

ULTRA would appear to make ground warfare easier than before, but the essential military problem was still there—the difficulty of precise communication. And without jeopardizing secret intelligence sources. That main military problem remains: rigorously exact communication between those at the top who know and those below who must act. What happens when this communication grows loose, fuzzy, or imprecise is illustrated by the disaster of COBRA. Focusing on the military importance of sheer speed, I once suggested that the West Point motto, "Duty, Honor, Country," might well be amended to "Duty, Honor, Celerity." Now, I'm not sure that the final word shouldn't be *Clarity*. (By the way, in the Pacific war, it was codebreakers' disclosure of the immense Japanese strengthening of the island of Kyushu, the planned first target of the American invasion, that had momentous consequences. This awareness of what the ground forces might face, many think, assisted the decision to end the war with atom bombs instead of boys wielding rifles.)

It is not pleasant to consider how awful the war against Germany would have been without FUSAG, Doublecross, and ULTRA. On D day especially, it was still hell. The heartrending events of Omaha Beach need no further description here, for by now they have been amply registered in histories, memoirs, and films. Speaking of which, I'd like to recommend the retention of and familiarity with the first few minutes of Steven Spielberg's *Saving Private Ryan* depicting the landing horrors. Then I'd suggest separating them to constitute a short subject, titled *Omaha Beach: Aren't You Glad You Weren't There?* Which could mean, "Aren't you glad you weren't a conscripted working-class or high school boy in 1944?" The rest of the Spielberg film I'd consign to the purgatory where boys' bad adventure films end up.

The FORTITUDE deception succeeded in fooling the Germans for a whole month, paralyzing their 15th Army waiting near Calais for the invasion there that never came. The Allies had duped them not just about the place of the invasion but the time as well, for they couldn't imagine an amphibious operation taking place in the terrible weather dominating the channel in early June. Secure in the belief that the invasion was not going to come soon, senior German officers went inland to participate in military exercises. "They won't come in this weather," an officer assured his subordinates, a small but telling illustration of the German military's liability to gullibility and self-deception, its innocence of irony, its will to believe, erected on the foundation of an illusionary national superiority, as Kenneth Macksey convincingly sets forth in his book *Why the Germans Lose at War.* But perhaps in view of intelligence failures like Pearl Harbor, the Bulge, 9/11, and even the collapse of the Soviet Union, gloating by us isn't appropriate.

The Boys and the French

General George S. Patton knew France quite well and was one of the few army commanders who could speak French—not fluently, to be sure, but satisfactorily. Henry James's *A Little Tour in France* would seem to have been known by him, for in his memoir *War As I Knew It,* he may be glancing at it in a sardonic section title, "Touring France with an Army." In a pamphlet about how to behave in France, American soldiers were advised that it would be well never to refer to the French defeat of 1940. (How could they have referred to it when they knew no French but *Voulez-vous couchez avec moi?* The very date 1940 would probably have floored most of them.)

"A country that means nothing to us"—GI Mitchell Sharpe's view of France was shared by most of the GIs. They had heard of France, certainly, but it is a fair bet that, high school education being what it was—and is—they had little acquaintance with Montaigne, Voltaire, or Flaubert, Cézanne, Matisse, or Monet. They were not familiar with the French intellectual and emotional style of tough disbelief and wry skepticism. Perhaps some clichés about food and sex were familiar, but details were rare, despite one GI on a truck carrying him toward Paris shouting joyously, "We're all going to get laid, French style!"

The ads bordering the roads certainly conveyed little to these boys. What meanings could be evoked by Bibendum, the Michelin Man; or the names of potables like St. Raphael, Pernod, Stella Artois, and Dubonnet? The red and white *bornes* marking every kilometer were a total novelty, and just about the only familiar brand name, for those who knew about sewing machines, was Singer. Houses seen from the road curiously lacked grassed front yards and were built of stone or brick, never wood. And it is certain that the troops had not seen before a pissoir on a city street.

Besides occasioning the enforced presence of American boys in this Oz-like place by egregiously losing the war against the Germans in 1940, there were other reasons for friction between French and Americans. After the Normandy invasion, the Americans had to equip an all-but-nonexistent French army with Sherman tanks and American uniforms, only slightly altered to bring them close to French tradition, like providing leaders with kepis for headwear. Watching Frenchmen dressed very like Yanks getting women as they flaunted GI garb on the streets was certainly annoying. And for their part, the French didn't at all appreciate the immense black market in Paris run by over two thousand American deserters. Nor could they forgive apparent carelessness about French lives when they totted up the damage wrought by American aircraft bombing and strafing everything handy in the Pas de Calais area. The same situation arose with the bombing constituting COBRA. General Bradley was informed that the use of heavy bombers would kill civilians and ruin their villages. Why not at least warn the inhabitants what was coming and let them take sensible shelter elsewhere? No. It was decided that to do so would alert the Germans to the disaster that was about to befall them. The point of the whole operation was to obliterate that part of the German army holding up the Allied advance, and that advance had to proceed, regardless of any humane complications.

Some French civilians tried to repress their instinctive

contempt for the Americans while the war was not yet won, but afterward there broke out what one soldier recalled as "an endless battle between native and GI." The locals sold the troops "dishonest bottles of wine." The GIs countered by throwing from their vehicles, in answer to begging cries for cigarettes and candies, used and ripe old condoms, "filled," said one soldier, "with our drainings."

But above all what was at issue was the discouraging fact that twice in one half century the Americans were required (as they conceived) to come and be killed fighting the same enemy so French chestnuts could be pulled from the fire. On the wall of a ruined fort in Verdun these eloquent words are said to appear:

> Austin White, Chicago, Ill., 1918
> Austin White, Chicago, Ill., 1945
> This is the last time I want to write my name here.

And one GI's view of Europe can stand for the feelings of virtually all: "This goddamn Europe. A thousand years of unending quarrels behind them, and they are still fighting. This place was a cesspool, beyond redemption. Why didn't the U.S. turn its back on them? Let them kill each other. Why should America sacrifice its young men in fruitless carnage?" There was no answer now, and no soldier believed there might ever be an answer.

An Episode Called Cobra

The month of July 1944 was profoundly discouraging for the Allies. After more than a month, their ground troops had not broken through the heavy crust confining them to little more than a beachhead in Normandy, and the planned breakout was far behind schedule.

The main problem was the landscape of the Bocage country of Normandy, which featured countless small agricultural squares separated by waist-high, thick earth walls. Hedgerows, these were called, and the Germans, who had plenty of time for preparation, developed powerful defensive positions out of them. The only way for the Americans to advance was to cross a series of these little overgrown walls, which operated like the trenches of the First World War. To appear unprotected by one was to be killed by rifle, machine gun, or tank fire, followed by grenades, mortars, and artillery. The difficulty of fighting in the hedgerows has generated a whole literature of anger, frustration, and savagery. For the attackers there seemed nothing to do but hunker down and wait for someone to provide a solution.

Someone finally did. Tanker sergeant Curtis G. Culin Jr. saw what was needed. He welded a large steel forklike thing to the front of a tank. This could be run into a hedgerow and toss up enough dirt to clear a passage, severely disheartening the enemy and clearing the way—until the next hedgerow, when the same performance would be repeated. This whole experience of the long holdup by the hedgerows illustrates that the Germans were as good at defense as the Americans were not. American strengths were in attack: airpower and rapid forward movement, and both were now called on for the ultimate breakout.

The immensity of the problem of breaking through the German defense can be appreciated by the immensity of the solution finally settled upon. It was as if the staff were guided by the aphorism of Oscar Wilde: "Nothing succeeds like excess." General Omar Bradley, who had authority to call upon the air corps in his area, decided to use fighter-bombers and heavy B-17 strategic bombers, usually used to destroy cities and the people within them, to open the way for a massive ground breakthrough. The German positions ran close to a road connecting the town of Périers with St. Lô. The road offered a six-kilometer stretch readily identifiable from the air. Bradley designated it and the space to each side of it, two kilometers wide, as the crucial landmark that would guide the planes. Earlier, in using heavy bombers this way as tactical weapons close to advancing troops, the hazards of friendly fire had proved discouraging. But the situation now was so close to desperate that the chance of a screwup was worth taking.

For safety the troops secretly withdrew a considerable distance from the front and the air corps understood that the planes would fly parallel with the road so they could keep on course by guiding along it. They also could avoid bombing the infantry by heeding cloth strips delineating the sides of the road and watching for pots of colored smoke marking the corners of the rectangle constituting the target.

The operation, denominated COBRA, was originally set for July 24, but heavy overcast forced cancellation—but not until many bombers, not hearing or not understanding the radio signal to abort, dropped their bombs and killed twenty-five infantrymen of the 30th Division who were preparing to jump off when the whistle blew. The pilots of the bombers, alas, had followed not a parallel but a perpendicular approach to the crucial road, violating, Bradley held, a firm agreement to fly along the road, not across it. That course would give the pilots a longer view of the target and a cleaner warning if they should not be over it. Bradley was furious at what he regarded as an unauthorized change in the aviators' tactics. But bombing from either approach would have been approximately as disastrous, because the smoke and dust of the bombs blotted out all land features, and the normally benign and unsuspected breeze moved the dust line over the American troops.

The next day, with command sensitivities of both air and ground forces in shock but with apologies and hopes to do better next time, the operation was tried again. Again, catastrophe, and even worse than the first time: 1,800 B-17s and 550 fighter-bombers, assisted by fire from 1,000 artillery pieces, killed 111 U.S. infantry and wounded almost 500. Friendly fire, with a vengeance.

Lieutenant Murray Pulver, of the 30th Division, was there with his men, ready to attack. But, as he says,

> I looked up to see that a wave of bombers had released too soon. My God, those bombs were going to hit us! We dove into our shallow slit trench. I started to pray.... I knew that we were all going to die. I began reciting the Twenty-third Psalm: "The Lord is my shepherd, I shall not want." . . . It came so clearly to me, as if I were reading from the Good Book. The earth trembled and shook.

Correspondent Ernie Pyle was there and he had a wider view of the disaster:

> There was still an hour before the bombers. . . . There was nothing for the infantry to do but dig a little deeper and wait. . . .
>
> The first planes of the mass onslaught came over a little before 10 A.M. . . . The main road running crosswise in front of us was their bomb line. They were to bomb only on the far side of that road.
>
> Our kickoff infantry had been pulled back a few hundred yards this side of the road. Everyone in the area had been given the strictest orders to be in foxholes, for high-level bombers can, and do quite excusably, make mistakes.
>
> We were still in country so level and with hedgerows so tall there was simply no high spot—either hill or building—where you could get a grandstand view of the bombing. . . .
>
> Having been caught too close to these things before, I . . . picked a farmyard about 800 yards back of the kickoff line.
>
> And before the next two hours had passed, I would have given every penny, every desire, every hope I've ever had to have been just another 800 yards further back.
>
> On time, dive bombers hit [the long rectangular target area] just right. . . .
>
> And then a new sound gradually droned into our ears. . . . It was the heavies. . . . They came in a constant procession and I thought it would never end. What the Germans must have thought is beyond comprehension. . . .
>
> I stood with a little group of men, ranging from colonels to privates, back of [a] stone farmhouse. Slit trenches were all around the edges of the farmyard and a dugout with a tin roof was nearby. But we were so fascinated by the spectacle overhead that it never occurred to us that we might need the foxholes.
>
> And then the bombs came. They began ahead of us as the

> crackle of popcorn almost instantly swelled into a monstrous fury of noise that seemed surely to destroy all the world ahead of us.
>
> From then on for an hour and a half that had in it the agony of centuries, the bombs came down. A wall of smoke and dust erected by them grew high in the sky. It filtered along the ground back through our own orchards. It sifted around us and into our noses. The bright day grew slowly dark from it. Some of the bombers were hit by German anti-aircraft fire and a few parachutes were seen. But nothing of that sort affected the bombers at all.
>
> Then we were horrified by the suspicion that those machines, high in the sky and completely detached from us, were aiming their bombs at the smokeline on the ground—and a gentle breeze was drifting the smokeline back over us!
>
> We dived. Some got in a dugout. Others made foxholes and ditches. . . .
>
> I was too late for the dugout. The nearest place was a wagon-shed. . . . I remember hitting the ground flat . . . and then squirming like an eel to get under one of the heavy wagons in the shed.
>
> There is no description of the sound and fury of those bombs except to say it was chaos, and a waiting for darkness. The feeling of the blast was sensational. The air struck you in hundreds of continuing flutters. Your ears drummed and rang. You could feel quick little waves of concussions on your chest and in your eyes.

The bombing finally over, Pyle turned to the state of the bombed American troops; and as was his wartime journalistic habit, he found grounds for good news:

> The leading company of our battalion was to spearhead the attack 40 minutes after our heavy bombing ceased. The company had been hit directly by our bombs. Their casualties, in-

> cluding casualties in shock, were heavy. Men went to pieces and had to be sent back. The company was shattered and shaken.
>
> And yet Company B attacked, . . . and within an hour they sent word back that they had advanced 800 yards through German territory and were still going.

Pyle concludes his story in characteristic style: "The American soldier can be majestic when he needs to be."

Censorship prevented Pyle from going into matters known to some of the officers present, like the appalling fact recorded by honest Russell Weigley, that many of the boys mangled or blown to bits were green replacements, "some . . . only several days out of Camp Walters, 21 weeks in the army from the time of their induction."

And a classic bit of disingenuousness was practiced by the Associated Press and Wide World Photos. It attached this caption to a battle picture depicting GIs frantically digging out their buddies from ruined foxholes: "After German shelling, Yanks dig out men buried in their foxholes."

Among the high-ranking officers who had assembled to view the bombing operation was Lieutenant General Lesley J. McNair, who had come over from England to watch. In England, he had been playing the fictive commander of the fictive FUSAG. General Patton had relinquished that role and moved secretly to Normandy to lead Third Army as it rushed forward to trample on the COBRA-destroyed German line and then kept moving, fast.

For years, General McNair had been specializing in training the new divisions that in due course would storm into France. In 1942, when he began his rugged pedagogy, the army ground forces numbered 700,000 men. By July

1943, the number was 2,200,000. Now, some distance behind the COBRA danger zone, he was going to observe from a foxhole the way the troops he'd trained had learned their lessons.

After the bombing had finally stopped, he couldn't be located. Hours later, an extended search found his mangled remains blown sixty yards from his foxhole. The body was identified by a piece of his collar bearing three stars.

And what was the effect on the enemy of this novel way of attacking? The Panzer Lehr Division, for one, was very badly beaten up. Trees were uprooted, rifle and machine-gun positions buried, tanks overturned. Some roads, including many required by the American attackers, simply disappeared. Craters were everywhere, some thirty feet across. Historian Martin Blumenson estimates that around one thousand German troops were killed by the bombing, and—this estimate might surprise infantry survivors—"only local and feeble resistance was possible against attacking American infantrymen."

During the bombing, some German troops, literally driven insane, blew out their brains rather than remain in the noise, the flame, the smoke, the screams, the shaking earth, the flying bodies and parts of bodies. Ordered from on high to "Hold in position," General Fritz Bayerlein replied, "My grenadiers and the pioneers, my anti-tank gunners, they're holding. None of them have left their positions, none. They're lying in their holes, still and mute, because they are dead. Dead. Do you understand?" A bit later, he reported, "After an hour I had no communication with anybody, even by radio. By noon nothing was visible but dust and smoke. My front lines looked like the face of the moon and at least 70 percent of my troops were out of action—dead, wounded, crazed, or numb." The Americans, for all they had suffered on their side, got the best of the bargain, for they did not become victims of a fierce ground attack while contemplating and cleaning up the sad mess left by the bombs. Two days later General Lawton Collins attacked with six divisions, two of them armored, and made rapid progress, penetrating the enemy rear so deeply that his soldiers killed a division commander, normally operating safely in the rear.

The COBRA disaster produced one other good effect: knowledge gained from the experience of using bombers to support ground troops. If the attacking army had enjoyed absolute, God-like control over weather, wind distance and direction, and general visibility, the fantastic operation might have come off as planned. But as the air corps' abandoning attempts at the "precision" bombing of Europe and taking up "area" bombing might have indicated, bombing could not be accurate. As the postwar U.S. Strategic Bombing Survey disclosed, aerial bombing accuracy was achieved more in advertising than in actuality.

Exposed as a result of the COBRA fiasco were the false promises of strategic aerial support of ground armies. The fantasy of smooth, rational victories at little cost was now a nightmare, and the infantry realized that the only way to win the war was to fight on and on and, if lucky, survive the inevitable wounds.

Tourists prowling around the COBRA area should not waste time looking for a memorial to the boys killed by the bombing error. There is none.

The Boys Hold Out Near Mortain

Released from stasis by COBRA, the American infantry and tanks made dramatic advances into France, and for a time there was a feeling in the air that the war was about to be won. For the moment, it was easy to forget that a central German tactical principle was immediate vigorous counterattack. If the American boys forgot it, Hitler did not, and as ULTRA informed Bradley, the Führer commanded the senior officer in the area, Field Marshal Gunther von Kluge, to press an instant tank counterattack beginning roughly at the town of Mortain and continuing for twenty-one miles along the coast to Avranches. If the attack was successful, it would envelop a considerable part of the Allied force and relieve German units gradually being chopped up by constant defensive actions.

Hitler's habit of uttering nonnegotiable orders from a great distance was perfect for ULTRA, and Bradley had almost nonstop recourse to that device in the following days. The German tankers must have wondered how the enemy fighter-bombers could locate their bivouacs so precisely; and the German infantry must have despaired of knowing how enemy artillery could find them and follow their movements so closely. Kluge, who had already had his troubles with Hitler, even to playing cat-and-mouse with those planning his assassination, was regaled with Hitler's deranged pep talks about the counterattack. When on the evening of August 7 Kluge reported that "the attack has been brought to a standstill by the loss of over half the tanks" and suggested that he break off the battle to save the remaining troops and Panzers, Hitler's unyielding reply reflected his customary monomania about "will," intensified now by his experience of Wehrmacht perfidy in trying to blow him up on July 20. He radioed Kluge: "I command the attack be prosecuted daringly and recklessly to the sea—regardless of risk. . . . Greatest daring, determination, imagination must give wings to all echelons of command. Each and every man must believe in victory." (Phrases like "I command," "give wings to," and "must believe" are pure Hitler, power nuttiness wedded to Viennese sentimentality.)

After a few days, Hitler declared, "with a harsh edge to his voice," as General Walter Warlimont recalled, that "the attack failed because Field Marshal von Kluge wanted it to fail." (Perhaps true, in a way, if the rumor can be believed that Kluge, when the counterattack was clearly not succeeding, left his headquarters mysteriously for a day, presumably to find an American general to surrender his front to. Hearing of this, Hitler relieved Kluge, who earlier had urged him to end the war, in favor of an enthusiastic Nazi. Kluge killed himself by biting into a cyanide capsule.)

American behavior during the six-day battle of Mortain has generated heroic narrative comparable with that attending the defense of the Alamo. But there is little doubt that the 2nd Battalion of the 30th Division's 120th Infantry Regiment, despite being badly damaged by the COBRA error, did an amazing job on this occasion. It managed to occupy and hold the most conspicuous high ground in the area, designated Hill 317. (The numbers on maps signified height above sea level.) This hill overlooked the main road running from Mortain to Avranches. Occupying it, the Americans could direct artillery fire onto the Germans, as well as the bombs and strafing machine guns of planes, not to mention the work of scores of RAF Typhoon fighter-bombers firing their rockets. Without possession of this hill, the Germans had little chance of fulfilling the mission laid down by Hitler and, at first, by Kluge. With repeated attacks, the Germans tried and tried to gain the hill. The Americans resisted solidly, and, some say, with bayonets fully serving their intended use, not merely employed as usual to goad prisoners or to scare Germans without penetrating them.

The Germans employed four Panzer divisions accompanied by SS troops who shouted *"Heil Hitler!"* as they attacked. The GIs had many bazookas, the rocket-firing tube deadly to tanks if a vulnerable spot could be hit, and the normal infantry weapons: rifles, machine guns, and mortars. They almost lost the struggle because their food and water ran out, and the batteries of their radios, crucial for adjusting artillery fire, grew so weak they had to be enlivened by being placed in hot sunlight for a while.

Lieutenant Ralph Kerley, commander of E Company of the 120th, would seem to personify the impudent spirit of the whole defense. A fellow officer described him as "kind of a loose cannon, a great combat leader, utterly fearless. He was rough, tough, unkempt, unshaven, profane, a heavy drinker and disdainful of red tape and protocol." But even these valuable characteristics became of little use as the battle wore on. Lieutenant Kerley said of August 9: "The ammunition supply had dwindled to almost nothing. Several of the severely wounded died during the night. The bodies of the dead, both our own and the enemy, were deteriorating fast in the warm August sun and the stench on the hill was nauseating." There were some hastily contrived airdrops of rations, water, and medical supplies, but most failed, delivering the goods into German hands. The 2nd Battalion of the 120th was adding meaning to the cliché of the Lost Battalion, surrounded but holding to the end. Although its position was quite known, no unit could strengthen it. A few of the radios could be encouraged to work well enough to coordinate with the fighter planes. Sadly idle during the foggy mornings, the planes became impressively active as the fog burned off, filling the road with burning tanks and trucks and half-tracks and screaming, writhing German infantry. Finally the 30th Division was relieved by the 35th, together with much armor. The enemy gradually retreated, taking several days for this process until by August 12, they were gone. The American 30th Division had lost more than 15 percent of its boys (3,516 of the division's infantrymen were killed before the war was over).

The defense of Hill 317 drew from Axis Sally, the German radio propaganda voice, an adjective much valued among the National Socialist military: *fanatisch* ("fanatical"). After the German defeat at Mortain, she referred to "the fanatical 30th Division, Roosevelt's SS troops." Not skillful, courageous, intelligent, et cetera, but *fanatical.* As the Germans began conspicuously to lose their battle in the West, the word appears increasingly in their vocabulary of praise and duty. Victor Klemperer has observed, "If someone replaces the words 'heroic' and 'virtuous' with 'fanatical' for long enough, he will come to believe that a fanatic really is a virtuous hero, and that no one can become a hero without fanaticism." Such Nazi diction suggests that language is all they had left, and that their mad attempt to reverse their impending defeat and shame really was fanatical in a more pejorative, even a clinical sense.

The Lost Opportunity at Falaise

The military indispensables of both celerity and clarity underwent a significant testing in the affair of the Falaise Pocket in the middle of August. Here, as Bradley was joyously aware, was a chance to capture or destroy the bulk of the German forces remaining in France. The chance was lost because—as the Americans thought—Montgomery, commanding Allied units at the north of the trap, was too slow making his dispositions, and his Canadian and Polish armored units were too green and clumsy to perform their assignment in time. And in the south a screwup of orders delayed Patton in his task of closing the bottom of the trap.

A way to visualize the scene is to posit a capital letter C. The arm on top is where the British, Canadians, and Poles were, near Falaise, in position to bring that arm together with the lower American one, fifteen miles southeast, near Argentan, making the C resemble an O, with the Germans helplessly enveloped inside. The movement of both arms had to be timely, but neither was, with the result that of the 100,000 Germans in the pocket, 40,000 escaped, fleeing east to reorganize and continue opposing the Allied advance.

Someone was clearly at fault in creating this missed opportunity, and of course the Americans, noting that Monty had assigned his least experienced Canadian and Polish armored units to the job, held that it was all his fault. The Canadians were relatively new to the European battle scene and were making sad goofs, like mistakenly shelling themselves and then taking too long in shock and shame to clear up the error. The matter of blame for the German escape remains undetermined. Military historian S.L.A. Marshall was probably right when, after considerable study, he concluded that the question can probably never be answered, but among the American rank and file, the matter has simplified itself into conclusions like those of the 30th Division historian Alwyn Featherston, who writes without doubt or qualification of "the British failure to close the Falaise Gap."

Instead of pursuing that question further, it may be more telling to consider the experience of the sixty thousand troops and civilians (the encirclement included half-populated agricultural fields) trapped in the pocket with no hope of relief. These became a handy, hardly missable target for the aircraft and artillery of the Americans, who had plenty of ammunition and who for days tormented relentlessly these German youths and men and French adults and children. This book is not intended as a pacifist text, but the appalling truth may be let out occasionally.

Oberfeldwebel (Master Sergeant) Hans Erich Braun recalls details of the scene:

> The never-ending detonations—soldiers waving to us, begging for help, the dead, their faces screwed up but still in agony—huddled everywhere in trenches and shelters, the officers and men who had lost their nerve—burning vehicles from which piercing screams could be heard—a soldier stumbling, holding back the intestines which were oozing from his abdomen—soldiers lying in their own blood—arms and legs torn off—others, driven crazy, crying, shouting, swearing,

> laughing hysterically. But also there were civilians lying by the roadside, loaded with personal belongings . . . and still clinging to them in death. Close by a crossroads, caught by gunfire, lay a group of men, women, and children. Unforgettable, the staring gaze of their broken eyes and the grimaces of their pain-distorted faces. Destroyed prams and discarded dolls littered the terrible scene.

Novelist Kingsley Amis, his comic outlook usually in faultless operation, was forced to sound a different note when his unit of British signals had to cross this shocking ground. Normally his section's mission obliged it to move forward daily and tediously set up its switchboards anew. Even this sort of military life entailed acute diarrhea,

> heavy continuous rain and arriving after dark in a field you had not seen in the light where no latrines had been dug, but it still beat being killed. I saw a lot of people whom that happened to around Falaise, so recently that there had been no time to bulldoze some to the roadside. Like life-sized dolls, everyone said, as everyone always has. The horses . . . seemed almost more pitiful, rigid in the shafts with their upper lips drawn above their teeth as if in continuing pain. The dead cows smelt worse. The stench of rotting human and animal bodies was so overpowering that the pilots of the spotter planes flying above the scene to direct more and more artillery damage vomited.

As German troops got close to the ever-shrinking escape areas, discipline tended to vanish and troops got as drunk as possible after slipping and sliding on the animal and human intestines on the roads. Panzer commander von Luck remembers:

> On 19 August came the order "Every man for himself." . . . We set out on the way to the east. At the sight of naked, half-burned tank men we promised ourselves that we would not let ourselves be finished off in the pocket. It was a hellish journey. . . . We had to abandon our tanks. We continued on foot. . . . The closer we got to the breakout point the more ghastly was the scene that met our eyes. The roads were blocked by two or three shot-up, burnt-out vehicles standing alongside each other, ammunition was exploding, tanks were burning. . . . In the fields far and wide was the same chaos. The enemy artillery fired into the turmoil from all sides. . . . In the afternoon of 21 August it was all over; the pocket was closed. How, if at all, could the men recover from this blood-letting and terrible experience?

Conclusive is the American Supreme Commander's comment, which is well known, or ought to be:

> The battlefield at Falaise was unquestionably one of the greatest "killing grounds" of any of the war areas. Roads, highways, and fields were so choked with destroyed equipment and with dead men that passage through the area was extremely difficult. Forty-eight hours after the closing of the gap I was conducted through it on foot, to encounter scenes that could be described only by Dante. It was literally possible to walk for hundreds of yards, stepping on nothing but dead and decaying flesh.

And Eisenhower is gentleman enough not to offend readers of his memoir *Crusade in Europe* by dwelling on the smell.

One Small-Unit Action

Not all the fighting and dying was as monumental as that of D day, COBRA, and the Falaise Pocket, or later the Hürtgen Forest and the Bulge. And not all GIs were like the boy angry that he had to risk his life fighting for France, "a country that means nothing to me."

A different and rare GI was Private First Class Robert Kotlowitz from Baltimore, a student at Johns Hopkins and the Peabody Conservatory of Music and a self-proclaimed Francophile. His origins were Polish-Jewish and he was highly intelligent with a valuable gift for subtle irony. As an enlisted man in the infantry he was an extraordinary item, so civilized as to be close to an anomaly. At Johns Hopkins he was a premed student, largely to avoid the draft. But racking up a series of D's and F's in this uncongenial discipline, he quit, and in 1943, at the age of eighteen, he was drafted. He was almost happy to be a soldier instead of a failing student. As he writes in his memoir *Before Their Time*,

> I believed in the war. It seemed just and righteous to me. In my simpleminded adolescent way, I hated the Nazis. I knew that terrible things were happening everywhere. I understood perfectly well, however many courses I may have failed, that I was living in a murderous century, one without pity and probably without precedent.
>
> I was ready to go.

After basic training, he was selected, like 150,000 other needlessly bright soldiers, to join the Army Specialized Training Program, which allowed enlisted men to attend universities and study engineering, mathematics, and languages. Attend, that is, until they were required as infantry replacements. Kotlowitz was sent to the University of Maine, but after a few months, the program was closed down and in April 1944, these favored youths were sent to infantry divisions. Their bitterness at this drastic demotion (many thought an actual promise had been made to keep them out of the physical and hazardous war) has lasted a lifetime. Kotlowitz's fate was the 26th Division, training at Camp Jackson, South Carolina, famous for its achievements in the First World War. "As soon as we arrived," says Kotlowitz, "we were sucked into the innards of the division, whose officers and non-commissioned officers could hardly believe their eyes when they saw us. New Meat, in their hungry words, fresh beef, and young (virginal, too, in most cases), a windfall of malleable human flesh when it was really needed." The immense number of infantry casualties so far had startled the staffs (why, one wonders; what did they expect?), and every experienced division was getting depopulated.

Kotlowitz's assignment was to the first squad of the third platoon of Company C, 104th Infantry. The commander of Company C was Captain Michael Antonovich (not his real name), and, says Kotlowitz, "I was not the only one with doubts about him. Everyone in the Company had them, including the non-commissioned officers." The main reason: the captain was not bright, but thought he was. Actually, the company was run by the first sergeant, Rene Archambault, while Antonovich devoted himself to screwing things up when he could. The captain "wasn't really intelligent enough to be a company commander—not that brilliance is needed for the job, although soundness is. As it was, the captain lacked both." Officers as bad as Antonovich were inevitable, given the difficulties of hastily accumulating an army of amateurs. Back in 1941, General McNair often expressed the view that "*Many* officers neither had nor deserved the confidence of their men" (my emphasis).

A very different sort of officer was the one leading Kotlowitz's platoon. If Antonovich was large and athletic, First Lieutenant Francis J. Gallagher was small, "with shanks like fishbones and a frame as delicate as a cobweb." He was largely unfrightened by angry higher ranks, and he delivered his frank views to them whenever opportunity offered. There were already signs of friction between lieutenant and captain, and "wisely enough, Gallagher and Antonovich kept their distance from each other. . . . When all else failed, as it often did in the Army, Antonovich tended to fall back on hysteria, like so many oversized men. While Antonovich screamed . . . , Gallagher, in the same situation, merely grew shrill."

Kotlowitz's squad (including one Browning Automatic Rifle team of three, and one corporal as second in command) was led by Rocky Hubbell. Kotlowitz and two other smart-ass ASTP transfers were of course assigned to the BAR team, which carried heavier and more clumsy loads than the mere riflemen. This was punishment for their assumed snobbery and former good luck. The squad included various oddities, one a thief of other men's underwear, another a silent boy from Vermont, "who spoke perhaps half a dozen sentences a day." When Kotlowitz joined the company, the 26th Division was on maneuvers near Nashville, "among the sodden Tennessee hills," along the Cumberland River. It was while on these maneuvers that Kotlowitz learned something about the unbridgeable distance separating military usages from those of ordinary, traditional life.

The maneuvers involved two divisions, and for the attacking division, Kotlowitz's, the problem was to enact a night river crossing in rubber boats and establish a bridgehead on the "enemy's" shore. The heavy mid-April rains kept the river full and sometimes angry and the troops wet and miserable, their leaking pup tents, for the four days they occupied them, providing little comfort.

"At two o'clock in the morning," says Kotlowitz,

> in a deluge, twenty YD [Yankee Division] infantrymen—at least half ASTP kids, median age nineteen—set themselves adrift, as planned, in a rubber assault craft from the turbulent southern shore of the Cumberland. The goal was to make it across to the other side . . . farther down the swollen river as part of an assault tactic that was one of the essential challenges of our maneuvers. . . .
>
> The twenty infantrymen, bowed deep under full equipment in their jammed rubber craft, kept swirling back to shore, spun by the current. There was almost no way to control the movement. All the previous crossings had faced the same problem, and they had solved it through stubbornly repeated tries and a certain amount of luck. . . . There has been no training, ever, in river crossings for the Yankee Division. So the attempt went on, out into the waters again for a second and a third time, until the vessel finally caught hold in mid-river and, spinning slowly, headed downstream, as hoped for.
>
> A few seconds passed as the assault boat disappeared into the dark. On shore, another twenty men from Company B moved into position, ready to board their own craft. Then, according to the evidence, there was a shout down-river from the assault boat, barely heard above the sound of the charging

waters, and another, soon followed by an eerie silence on both the river and the shore.

Then, senior officers on the shore began to perceive that they were present not at an exercise but a disaster. "Everything had suddenly gone crazily awry."

> "Facts" began to seep in, claims, contradictions, exaggerations, tall tales, horror stories; believed, not believed, accepted, rejected—the old chaos, reinforced by a powerful new reality. Nothing, however, was seen again that night of the men and the adolescent boys who tried to make the crossing. They had vanished almost without warning, in the unpenetrable darkness, sunk apparently by the heavy weight of the ordinary infantry equipment they were carrying. It was over in seconds: twenty bodies instantly drowned in fast-running water—a swift and terrible death, in full awareness.

Kotlowitz and his fellow infantrymen were seriously demoralized by the Cumberland calamity, to be sure, but there was something almost worse, a presage of further encounters with the unmentionable. The Cumberland scandal, Kotlowitz writes, "was never publicly acknowledged, never discussed with us in any official way, never reviewed with the line troops who might have learned something from it." Not only was there no public recognition that something terrible had happened; there was no elegy, no prayer, no placing of memorial pebbles on headstones. One of the lost, Moose Monchick, had been a pal of Kotlowitz's in the ASTP, and "I grieved for him," he says, alone and silently, with no ritual or anything like it (even information) to cushion the shock and sorrow.

On the day the 26th Division underwent a final review

before shipping overseas, writes Kotlowitz, "We thought about the Cumberland crossing a lot. . . . It had become a talisman of disaster in the Yankee Division, a bleak reminder of what could happen to any of us in the future. The message it delivered was stern, and we read it clearly and well."

—

Two months after D day, the 26th Division sailed from Brooklyn to join the Great Crusade. After ten days of zigzagging across the Atlantic, their ship arrived at the ruined port of Cherbourg, and the boys came ashore in Higgins boats, just like the real heroes of D day. Kotlowitz and his buddies were soon under tents in Calvados country, awaiting their next move. In this bivouac, they were bored repeatedly by Captain Antonovich's idiotic "lectures" on the distinction of the American Middle West, from whence he had emerged. The 26th Division was said to be waiting to join Lieutenant General William H. Simpson's Ninth Army, not yet completely organized. While Antonovich bored his listeners silly, Lieutenant Gallagher was doing the same with his lectures on infantry tactics. One thing he dealt with was the riskiness of frontal assaults, but he also covered flanking maneuvers and similar topics already thoroughly exhausted in the tedious training the troops had undergone.

As the men observed the nearby civilians, it became clear that the French regarded their liberators with something close to hatred, much of it doubtless due to the damage and death caused by the extensive preinvasion bombings of their property. But a lot of the hatred could be imputed to French contempt for non-French-speaking strangers invading their country to oppose other strangers they themselves had not been able to repel in 1940. The sight of a bald young woman living near the troops' bivouac suggested further French troubles, those occasioned by the desire for revenge against "collaborators," even the lonely girls too friendly with German soldiers. Whatever the cause, the Army of the United States seemed to regard all the French as "Out of Bounds, Off-limits, not to be spoken to, not to be approached or touched, as though they, and not the Germans, were the real enemy."

The waiting period before entering the fighting made the boys' silent focus on certain subjects inevitable. Fear was the main one. "Nobody wanted to talk about being scared. Our pride and self-esteem were involved, indeed threatened, and beyond that, we had no useful vocabulary to describe such a state. How do you talk about fear when fear is fast becoming the chief currency of life?"

The boys distracted themselves from considering that unattractive topic by dwelling on the visible friction between Antonovich and Gallagher, who very soon were going to have to lead them, not just into the valley of the shadow of death, but safely through it. Considerable hostility between the two could be predicted, especially after one incident when the two had disagreed, loudly and angrily, in front of the whole company. Just after the morning formation, Antonovich, apparently continuing an earlier quarrel, shouted to Gallagher, "It's just not revelant." Gallagher took plenty of time to make his audience eager for his reply. Then he shouted back, "The word is 'relevant.'" He began to walk away. "But the hell with it." The men, says Kotlowitz, were "unsettled" by this dual display of anger. "Nobody was happy to have witnessed it," and if anyone in the company had been skilled in foretelling the future, this unseemly performance in front of the men could seem a clear presage of later disaster. Soon, after an offensive, humiliating medical "short arm" inspection of penises and anuses, sudden action: the 26th Division was to proceed at once by trucks to join not Simpson's Ninth Army but Patton's Third, in the northeastern French area (former province) of Lorraine.

Thus, in early October the 26th Division entered the line, near Lunéville, relieving the 4th Armored Division. Lunéville (to the troops, Looneyville) is nineteen miles southeast of the city of Nancy, an occasional headquarters of General Patton. Kotlowitz and his fellows were pleased to note that they had no need to dig foxholes; they could use those left behind by the 4th Armored. Kotlowitz settled into a comfortable two-man hole with Roger Johnson, another member of the BAR team.

All went well until October 12, D day for the unblooded company. Lieutenant Gallagher's platoon was ordered to attack at dawn a small rise constituting for the Germans a slight and probably harmless little salient protruding into the American position. It was something the 4th Armored Division had been content to leave alone for some time, but now for some reason it was to be attacked and reduced. To get the job done, Gallagher's platoon assumed a diamond formation, with the lieutenant at the head. "There was no discussion of tactics," nor of the folly of an unsupported frontal attack on an unstudied position. "There were barely any orders. There wasn't time." The diamond haltingly moved forward, the boys "half blind with fear." Justified fear, for

> within a few moments, . . . a lot had happened. Lieutenant Gallagher, for one, was already dead. We saw him die, quickly. A bullet pierced his scrawny boy's neck . . . as he moved forward ahead of us, just over the top of the rise. . . . Someone

yelled Kaputt! as though it was an order. Gallagher stood there, upright and motionless, his ferret's face full of surprise, when the Germans began to fire their Mausers. At the same moment, perfectly synchronized, a 180-degree sweep of machine-gun fire, which at first I mistook for our own, took us from right to left . . . dropping the platoon where it stood. It then came around in a second sweep.

I saw a hole open up in the back of Lieutenant Gallagher's neck, when the bullet passed through the front—surprised at how large and black it was, clean, too, as though it had been drilled by a mechanic's precision tool. There was a surge of surface blood at first, then a gurgle, like a tap being turned on, then a sudden torrent as he fell without a sound. Both of his carotid arteries must have poured in one stream through the wound. All of this took perhaps a dozen seconds: Gallagher's death, the machine-gun assault, and the paralysis of the third platoon.

We lay on the ground without moving. It was now light. . . . The sounds . . . never before heard, swelling over the noise of small-arms and machine-gun fire, of boys' voices calling for help or screaming in pain or terror—our own boys' voices, unrecognizable at first, weird in pitch and timbre.

Deprived now of a leader to give orders, there seemed nothing to do but lie there—when the mortars began, and then the grenades, and then the

snipers, whose main job was to pick off our wounded: easy work that day, for each target was already immobilized. . . . There was no response that day from the rest of C Company behind us, no answering artillery or heavy weapons fire, and no supporting troops to help us slip out of the . . . rise that we had trapped ourselves in. The company hung tight somewhere in the rear for reasons of its own, never explained by Captain Antonovich or Master Sergeant Archambault, both

> of whom had somehow managed to escape this trip. . . . I thought of them bitterly and cursed them both for pigs.
>
> Slowly then, as the morning wore on, and the knowledge began to sink in, I came to realize that for us there was nothing to do but wait, flat out as we were, for our own deaths.

The only choice for Kotlowitz was to play dead by severely limiting his breathing—for twelve hours. He knew this was his only hope when one of the men suddenly got up and ran toward the rear. Machine-gun fire immediately brought him down.

Various awful cries, for help, water, and mother, indicated that all were not dead yet, but many died during the afternoon while Kotlowitz continued painfully simulating a corpse. At one point German commands could be heard, followed by a very long silence; then, as it grew dark, the whispers of American medics carrying their stretchers.

"Don't move," one medic said, as a cramp in Kotlowitz's leg became almost unbearable. He'd not urinated all day, and as he moved his leg and stood up, he "took a full minute to piss." Soon he could walk and help a medic carry a body on a stretcher. It was a long trip back. "My cramped leg hurt. . . . I wanted a cigarette. By the time we got back to company headquarters, perhaps five hundred yards to the rear, I was visibly trembling. . . . I couldn't stop." He wanted to be carried back to the division hospital "as though I had been respectably wounded. . . . But I was intact and unbloodied, and a little contemptuous of myself for it." He couldn't stop the trembling, and in the command tent he beheld the following:

> 1. Antonovich in hysterics, crying and moaning, trying to give an impression of innocence, sympathy, and understanding.

2. A and B Company commanders, together with a couple of lieutenants, visibly embarrassed.
3. A major, "looking angry but not saying a word."
4. "Two stupid-looking MPs."

The dominant sound was supplied by Antonovich, who clearly had to say something in defense of his own ineptitude—and his cowardice in not providing for the rescue of the endangered platoon. What he chose to say, and repeatedly, was "sweet Jesus," while waving his hands before his face. And then, noticing Kotlowitz, a pitiable attempt at expiation: " 'Get this man's name down, somebody. Put this man in for a silver star. I want that in the records, in writing. I want it in C Company's record. . . . Ah, sweet Jesus' and so on and so on for a while. . . ."

"Just get me out of here," Kotlowitz finally said, and still shaking and disoriented, he was put into a medical jeep. When at the hospital a chaplain made the sign of the cross over the jeep, Kotlowitz began crying, and he cried until finally an injection made him go to sleep. Later, he learned that in his 3rd Platoon, close to forty men had been killed, that is, virtually all of them, including its leader. The whole awful episode illustrates a frontline truism every unit had to learn: it took up to six weeks for a unit to learn to stay alive by abandoning most of the tactical knowledge instilled by stateside training.

At the division hospital, Kotlowitz found, "I was something new in the Yankee Division, a combat survivor, a rare specimen. . . . The division's historian wanted to talk to me." Kotlowitz was also attended to by the division's psychiatrist, and imagines his report on this interesting patient: "Sole unwounded survivor of engagement at or near Bézange-la-petite . . . normal guilt feelings at survival, combined with powerful frustrated aggression resulting from twelve-hour siege, during which time soldier did not fire a single round of ammunition at the enemy."

Adjudged finally a victim of combat fatigue, or something like it, he was sent, whether for therapy or punishment wasn't clear, to help guard a beat-up warehouse in the city of Nancy. It contained the Yankee Division's duffel bags, installed there while the troops fought the war in combat equipment. These duffel bags were to be carefully searched when their owners were killed lest something embarrassing be sent home. Though rat-infested, this "depot" was warm and safe, if constantly a target for black-marketeers and thieves. Kotlowitz's worst moment came with the order to locate in the thousands of duffel bags the ones belonging to the dead of the unfortunate 3rd Platoon of C Company, 104th Infantry.

A question remains: Who conceived and ordered this half-witted little attack led by poor Lieutenant Gallagher? Surely not Gallagher, too sensible and without sufficient authority. Perhaps Captain Antonovich, acting on directions from battalion or regimental operations officers, new to combat and anxious to look good by issuing orders to "straighten out the line."

Kotlowitz's interrogation by the division historian produced nothing useful to historiography or military theory. *The History of the 26th Yankee Division, 1941–1945* deals with the problem this way: "On October 12, C Company [of the 104th Infantry] attacked Hill 264 at Bézange-la-petite, and E Company wound up the fracas, seizing and securing the hill." This was after the Germans had left, bringing a safe and honorable conclusion to the now nonexistent "fracas."

Did Antonovich choose Gallagher to lead this stupid attack intending a degree of revenge for the earlier humiliation in front of his entire company? It was a not unknown practice for battalion and company officers to select "undesirable" officers to lead especially hazardous actions as a payback for slights, discourtesies, disparagement, or silent contempt, what the British army calls "dumb insolence."

Gallagher's bold correction of Antonovich's *revelant* may have triggered the whole thing. But the folks at home would know only that their eighteen-year-old boy had been killed "in action."

The Haunted Wood: Hürtgen Forest

If today an eighty-year-old survivor of the Boys' Crusade were asked to indicate his worst moment as an infantryman, he might answer "Omaha Beach." And then as an afterthought, he would be likely to add, "No, Hürtgen Forest"—less publicized and ciné-dramatized but equally unforgettable, at least for the few participants still living.

The "battle" of the Hürtgen Forest consumed most of the month of November 1944, and, as numerous observers and historians agree, it did not significantly shorten the war despite outrageous casualties: of the 120,000 boys who fought there, 33,000 were killed or wounded or went back sick or were driven insane. A great many officers, thought to have failed by showing insufficient "drive," were relieved and disgraced.

The theater of all this was a piece of land near Aachen of approximately fifty square miles. It comprised a variety of militarily horrible terrains: dark forests, stone ridges, deep gorges. This "hideous battleground," as Russell Weigley calls it, illustrated all at one time the deficiencies of the American system of troop replacement, the insufficiencies of American troop training, the failure of American divisional leadership, the innocence or ignorance of large-unit tactics by corps and army commanders, supply and imagination failure resulting in the absence of appropriate cold-weather uniforms, and unjustified staff optimism, the result of basing decisions on rear-echelon map study and rumors instead of actual visits to division, not to mention battalion, fronts.

Appalling as this protracted mess was, its context made it seem worse. It came at one of those moments when the United States, shocked already by the casualty totals, decided that the war had to become "better"—more progress, fewer dead and wounded. When any event suggested that the war might be over in a few weeks, the public allowed itself to grasp at the hope. And suddenly and surprisingly, their infantry boys were thrust into this thoroughly horrible situation, comparable, as many have said, to the scene of the First World War's Passchendaele. For those in the know, the horror of Hürtgen could be read in the number of self-inflicted wounds and the unprecedented rates of desertion. It was a desperate moment on the western front when, to halt the increasing desertions, pitiable serial deserter Private Eddie Slovik was formally shot to death in the only execution for desertion in the whole European Theater.

At the time, this attack was said to be in aid of the right flank and rear of the troops trying to reach the two large dams of the river Ruhr to prevent the Germans from flooding the Ruhr Valley, the Americans' next objective.

In the vast area of the forest itself, the Germans had dug in and wired and built log and dirt bunkers, exploiting the months since June, during which time they had had ample time to strengthen this part of the fortresslike West Wall, known also as the Siegfried Line, in preparation for the hard battle they knew was bound to come. Their prime defense was the nature of the forest itself. The immense fir trees, seventy to a hundred feet tall, were closely packed and kept the interior of the forest dark at all hours. The pine needles thick on the ground provided a perfect hiding place for antipersonnel mines—antitank mines were rare because the forest had insufficient open space for tanks. With easier address to all the American troops in the forest and a bit more torment from the weather and the enemy, someone adept at rhetorical appeal and organization might have generated an actual mutiny.

"Officially," the American in charge of all this was Lieutenant General Courtney H. Hodges, commander of First Army. He was running the battle from Spa, in Belgium, thirty miles away. At his best he must have been calm and impressive, but, as a military thinker, he was, says one historian, a "most conservative tactician, forever worried about his flanks." Having commanded a machine-gun company in the earlier world war and having experienced the Argonne, he might have been familiar with the special problem of fighting in a forest, where the troops cannot see the signals of the leader. On his visits to the line, he didn't often get farther forward than a division headquarters, and he was thus out of contact with the troops who had to obey his orders. He was innocently violating one of General Patton's wise observations: "Plans should be made by those who are going to execute them." Hodges had not exactly lost touch with his soldiers, but he seemed not to realize that he was commanding not professional troops but terribly scared boy draftees. Hodges brought to the battle a bundle of conventional approaches, while the battle demanded nothing but the unconventional. His corps commanders kept sending into the Hürtgen area division after division to replace those that had failed. The 28th Division was one of the first assigned to this hell. It failed, like the 9th Division it relieved. Next was the 8th Division, so badly mauled that it too had to be withdrawn, to be relieved by the 1st Division. Beaten up in turn, it yielded the job to the 4th Division. Then the 83rd Division. Then the 5th Armored. More than a quarter of all these troops became casualties, and what shell fragments, bullets, grenades, mines, and trench foot didn't take care of, diarrhea did.

These varied troops were brave enough and willing enough, but their experience in the forest was so awful that it produced a whole parade of "unmanly" behaviors: unordered flight and even rout; flagrant disobedience; bursting into tears; faking illnesses; and self-inflicted wounds. Here is radioman George Barrette's reaction to his first artillery barrage: "Me and this buddy of mine were in the same hole with only a little brush on top, and I remember I was actually bawling. We were both praying to the Lord over and over again to please stop the barrage, shaking and shivering and crying and praying all at the same time."

One cause of troop weakness was training failure: despite Lesley McNair's efforts, apparently no one had thought very hard about tactics to be used in heavy woods and defensive measures to be taken in such a setting. Apparently no officer or noncom had ever lectured on tree bursts, and there were few other kinds in a forest. (A tree burst is a shell burst not at ground level but up in the air. At ground level, a foxhole or trench will offer some protection, for the shell fragments come horizontally. But a tree burst delivers the fragments downward, and the only protection is to hug a tree.) One of Patton's maxims was, "Do not dig slit trenches under trees, if you can avoid it." Yes, but where else in this thick, dark forest could you find protection from shells bursting everywhere?

Not the most trustworthy division was the 28th, formerly the main infantry unit of the Pennsylvania National Guard. Able historian David Eisenhower, not given to exaggeration, writes that the 28th was a "problem" division known for desertions (it was Eddie Slovik's unit) and self-inflicted wounds. In one attack in early November, the 2nd Battalion of the 28th's 112th Regiment assaulted a difficult ridge in the Hürtgen. After a particularly severe German barrage "the men suddenly could stand no more," writes Charles B. MacDonald. "Panic-ridden, the men of one company grabbed wildly at their equipment and broke for the rear. . . . The impulse to run was a disease, a virulent, highly contagious disease that spread like the plague. Once started, the men would not stop," even when confronted by the pistols and carbines of officers ordering a halt. Of another failed 28th Division attack, MacDonald writes,

> Squads and platoons got lost; mortar shells landing among assault teams carrying explosive charges set off the explosives and blew up the men; an unfailing chatter of machine guns ripped through the trees when anyone moved. One man, a replacement, sobbing hysterically, tried to dig himself a hole in the ground with his fingers. In late afternoon this battalion . . . staggered back to the line of departure.

The commander of the 28th Division was the worthy Major General Norman Cota, promoted from brigadier general because of his intelligent and courageous behavior on the Normandy beaches. He did his best, which was notably good, but by the time of Hürtgen Forest his units were so loaded with boy replacements that his command could no longer shine. One artillery lieutenant wrote home on November 22 about trying to take the town of Schmidt: "We did not take it. We were cut to pieces, slashed to ribbons. This division as now constituted is not the old Twenty-eight. All new men. The old are mostly dead. . . ."

During the fighting in the Hürtgen, General Cota was said to be getting tired of visiting the front and seeing "all those empty holes" left by the numerous deserters.

The war over, the 28th Division, still in Europe, issued a public relations booklet for its members to send home, bragging about its achievements but maintaining a decent silence about its disasters. *28th Roll On: The Story of the 28th Infantry Division* is in its way a masterpiece—of omission, evasion, and cheerful euphemism, and necessarily so: How do you inform a proud mother about the body of a high school boy blown apart and left in snow and ice in the midst of unattended-to mines and booby traps? At the beginning of this little booklet, the soldier owner, presumed to be proud and cheerful, is invited to fill in blanks about his training and battle actions, making him complicit in lies and optimism too. At the end of this item, General Cota provides a cheerful message glancing obliquely at embarrassments like the Hürtgen Forest disaster: "Our successes have not as a rule come easily; however, because of skillful, determined and courageous effort, they have always been sure"—and thus the sentence tapers off into nonmeaning.

Aware of the horrors of Hürtgen, General Bradley tried the bomber solution again and had a thousand heavy bombers of the Eighth Air Force drop over four thousand tons on the German defenders. But because of the COBRA disaster, this time the bomb line was set so far in front of the American troops that, despite some damage, German skill at digging in deprived the attack of its hoped-for power.

One notable aspect of the Hürtgen Forest fighting is the way it could be accommodated to the imaginations and memories of the boys familiar with the Grimm brothers' folktales about ominous or mystical forests. Weigley thinks of the setting in something like the Grimms' terms when he speaks of "a witches' caricature of a forest," and John Ellis talks of fighting in forested mountains as "attacking a particularly intractable maze, but one inhabited by a malevolent breed of troll." For many, the forest possessed the attributes W. H. Auden in 1939 recalled scaring him in childhood when he had nightmares of being lost in a haunted wood. Baffled by the cause of one 28th Division failure, General Cota went forward but couldn't find a clue. "What was the matter now?" wonders Charles B. MacDonald. "Did the Hürtgen Forest foster some psychological malaise affecting soldier and commander alike?"

As the unspeakable days of November gave way to winter, with freezing weather, sleet, and snow, those on the line became aware that they weren't properly dressed for this affair: they'd not been issued warm winter clothing, including white camouflage garments. Their foxholes filled with water, which then froze, and in the absence of dry socks and boots, trench foot became common, half-welcomed because a severe case got a soldier off the line for a bit, although at the risk of having one or both feet amputated.

While stopping short of considering whether General Hodges had lost his mind, no one focusing on the matter of the Hürtgen Forest has been able to regard it as anything but an inexplicable catastrophe, begun, says Stephen E. Ambrose, "on the basis of a plan that was grossly, even criminally stupid." Why did Americans imagine they could win a struggle without use of the advantages that had brought success so far—their air corps, their mobility, their artillery adjusted by Piper Cub spotter planes viewing the ground below, but here unable to locate the enemy hidden in the forest? Russell Weigley is among the many puzzled over the Americans' curious First World War, infantry-only tactics: "An army that depended for superiority on its mobility, firepower, and technology should never voluntarily give battle where these assets are at a discount: the Hürtgen Forest was surely such a place." Weigley also stresses the oddity of Hodges's violation of the well-tried tactic of concentration of strength. "What is remarkable," he writes, "is the perseverance of the First Army in throwing one division after another into the dark maw of the Hürtgen Forest on extended fronts" and never concentrating all strength at one point. Why did division commanders persist in shoehorning inadequately trained, lonely kid replacements into units already severely troubled? Why did they not know the special problems of forest fighting, especially at night? Even in daytime, some boys among attacking troops had to use compasses to maintain the right direction. General James M. Gavin sums it all up with his sympathetic question, "How could they have gotten themselves into such a predicament?"

The blunders and horrors are vivid a half century later, and there are still survivors whose anger at the whole business will never cool—anger not, as the innocent might like to believe, at those formally designated their enemies, but at their own commanders who insisted on and presided over this conscienceless mess. Not a one resigned in a fury.

When in 1944 Thanksgiving Day was approaching, Dwight Eisenhower, for the sake of morale, which he knew was slipping, ordered that every soldier on the line be given a complete hot Thanksgiving dinner, regardless of the logistical difficulties of providing it. So in heavy rain, the troops in their foxholes ate their cold turkey dinners from water-filled mess kits, as if this were just one more mockery. One survivor, an ex-major of infantry, witnessed the slaughter of his battalion on that Thanksgiving Day. It is reported by Charles Whiting that he could never again eat a Thanksgiving dinner at home. He "would get up and go to the backyard and cry like a baby."

Replacements and Infantry Morale

If a draftee was bright, one of the first blows to his morale upon arriving at a camp for basic training must have been the message delivered by the letters R.T.C., visible everywhere. He quickly learned that they stood for Replacement Training Center. *Training* was clear enough, and so was *Center,* but *Replacement?* Why, he wondered, were so many hundreds of thousands of drafted boys needed as replacements? For whom or what? Was the army expecting that many deaths or incapacitating wounds?

Well, yes, it was, and since it couldn't totally conceal this knowledge from the victims-to-be, it came right out with it. The bright boy then must have wondered: Will a boy like me be killed or torn up or otherwise rendered unable to go on with the battle, to be replaced by me, probably to undergo the same experience in my turn?

The word *replacement* enjoyed a brief euphemistic elevation to *reinforcement* in late 1944, but this didn't take, and *replacement* remained the unavoidable, anxiety-making term.

In November 1944, when casualties in France were adding up, General Eisenhower issued an order making it possible for infantry units to look into the dark and horrible future and estimate the number of killed and wounded expected in the next forty-eight hours so that replacements could be made in timely fashion.

A replacement's arrival at a rifle company usually occasioned in him a sad collection of emotions, ranging from deep cynicism to outright terror. If he was lucky, a company commander gave him a hurried welcome and urged him to keep his head down and obey his squad and platoon leaders. He was then installed in a depleted squad, whose members seldom learned his name although they could identify him by a designation like Iowa, Pittsburgh, or Shorty. One young master of irony said of his assignment to an infantry platoon: "There wasn't a lot of companionship." And once installed, the replacement began to master the facts of infantry life, nicely articulated by infantry veteran Charles Reis Felix: "Nobody gets out of a rifle company. It's a door that only opens one way, in. You leave when they carry you out, if you're unlucky, dead, or if you're lucky, wounded. But nobody just walks away. That was the unwritten law."

One problem with replacements was that they hadn't yet accepted the virtual inevitability of forthcoming damage to their flesh and were sometimes conspicuously cowardly. Official army history does not bother to euphemize such moments except for its use of the term *retired* where someone else might say *fled* or *ran away* (in army idiom, *took off* or *hauled ass*). One sadly memorable moment was experienced by troops of the 90th Division in an attack, as Martin Blumenson reports: "In the pitchblack darkness, some of the demoralized troops began furtive movement to the rear. Stragglers, individually and in groups, drifted unobtrusively out of the battle area. Soldiers pretended to help evacuate wounded, departed under the guise of messengers, or sought medical aid for their own imagined wounds." At one of the worst moments for the reputation of the general, average infantry replacement, "despite little firing and few Germans in evidence, a group of American soldiers started toward the enemy, their hands up, some waving white handkerchiefs." And the problem was by no means limited to the 90th Division. The 83rd Division, because of its large intake of replacements, remained palpably unfit for some time, until it trained the newcomers itself.

Unless military planning and training is almost as brutal and cynical as battle itself in attending to the nature of man, unless replacement troops are trained rigorously and prepared psychologically, disaster is likely to occur.

In the Second World War, the shortage of infantrymen, visible as early as the Sicilian campaign, resulted in part from the innocence and credulity of the planners. They had invested too much belief in the assumption (easily credited because of the appalling massacres of the First World War) that this time, machines would do much of the infantry's work. This age was assumed to be more rational and sensitive than the one that destroyed a generation of foot soldiers in the Great War. We now had tanks, half-tracks, improved artillery, and an air corps to do much of the fighting that was once the job of the Poor Bloody Infantry.

This time the more intelligent conscripts were to be sequestered in the ASTP. Once the war ended, the United States would have an undamaged stratum of talent. Henry Stimson, Roosevelt's secretary of war, whose idea the ASTP was, thought it wise in this world war to give the better sort of people something more elevated to do than shooting others from mudholes.

All was fine until casualties among the ground forces surprisingly mounted. In haste, lads were rudely removed from their safe ASTP berths and thrust into the battered rifle companies. How angry they were at their government's apparently violating its promises! And anger was felt not by them alone. The air corps found itself overstocked with cadets fantasizing commissioned status. Seventy-one thousand of them had their program canceled and from nirvana were plunged into hell: they became infantry replacements and were sent to the hardest-hit divisions, like the 1st, the 3rd, the 4th, and the 29th. In their infantry companies, they were buddyless and shunned as almost dangerous strangers. These embittered replacements were a most pitiable group, lonely, despised, and untrained, deeply shocked by the unexpected brutalities of the frontline and often virtually useless.

The 90th Infantry Division offers examples. Of one disastrous operation historian Martin Blumenson says, "The main cause for failure was the presence of so many inadequately trained replacements." A staff sergeant commanding a platoon tells James Jones the sort of welcome replacements might expect when joining an already cohesive group:

> One day at Anzio we got eight new replacements into my platoon. We were supposed to make a little feeling attack that same day. Well, by next day, all eight of them replacements were dead. . . . But none of us old guys were. We weren't going to send our own guys out on point in a damnfool situation like that. We had been together since Africa, and Sicily, and Salerno. We sent the replacements out ahead.

That experienced sergeant's motive seems to be one largely unanticipated by higher echelons. While drawing up tables of organization and elementary guides to tactics, they appear to have neglected a sufficient study of actual human behavior. But sometimes by luck or skill, replacements did survive. Artilleryman Donald J. Willis wrote in 1945, in the awful winter of that year,

> Replacements reach us but we are still under-strength. They are very young and are confused and scared. No wonder, being thrust into a savage no-man's land, under the worst possible weather conditions. These young boys will know in a few days the horrible fatigue of the front-line soldier. Also the dragging step and the glazed eyes that see only enemy . . . The clean, sharp boy with new clothes . . . will be changed. In his place will be a man who at times will not look or act human at all. Like the rest of the spearhead soldiers, they will be dirty, frostbitten, and tired as they have never been before.

The boys Willis is thinking of are rare, for few lived so long. A repeated experience among platoon and company commanders was seeing a replacement killed or taken from the line wounded before they knew his name. Such could only be addressed as "soldier."

—

It took most of the ground war for leaders to realize that the threat of shame and contempt before an audience of valued intimate acquaintances was more powerful than patriotism or ideology or hatred of the enemy in exacting uncowardly behavior from soldiers. Trained at home among friends as they may have been, replacements entered the line as individuals, knowing no one. Missing was their critical audience of buddies whose disapproval they feared more than anything. How did this idea arise of inserting infantrymen singly as strangers into experienced units? It could make sense only to someone trained in business methods. As Michael Doubler writes, "Although the replacement system made good bureaucratic sense and promoted efficient management, it is hard to imagine a system more detrimental to the individual soldier's discipline, morale, and training." That is, thoroughly inhumane, as if thought up by the staff of a second-rate business school. One experienced infantryman noted, "Casualties come in bunches, like grapes." And it is in bunches, where the grapes are already familiar with one another, that they should be replaced.

General Joseph W. Stilwell, after his depressing experience in China trying to talk sense and honesty into Generalissimo Chiang Kai-shek and his wife, proposed a solution to the worst defect of the infantry-replacement system: train replacements and transfer them always in four-man groups, all buddies of long standing.

But a problem remains: wounds and death happen to individuals, not generally to bands of buddies with replacement groups waiting in the wings.

One irony of this highly modern war was that the Allied ground army grew worse as the war proceeded, at the same time the enemy (what remained of it) grew more intensely anxious not to be defeated, its fears and determination increasing near the end of the war by the hysterical fear of the Soviets planted by Joseph Goebbels and the practice among SS commanders of hanging reluctant troops with placards fastened to them reading, "I made defeatist remarks."

As early as 1943, leaders of the ground forces engaged in Southern Italy began to perceive a serious problem of morale. An official voice described the situation genteelly: "Fall rains and mountainous terrain make forward movement difficult," an understatement omitting reference to German mines and blown bridges. As the troops contemplated many months of hacking their way up the Italian peninsula, their cheerfulness was hard to sustain. Perhaps a special badge like the navy submariner's or the air corps' wings or the parachutist's decoration could be devised to make infantrymen think better of themselves, despite the gloomy facts. Thus the invention of the Expert Infantryman's Badge, awarded at "graduation" to men who completed training, and an advanced version, the Combat Infantryman's Badge, to be worn only by those who had gone on to experience mortal encounters with the enemy. (Perhaps the inspiration for this decoration came from the Close Combat Badge, which German troops had been wearing before the idea arrived in America.) The expert's badge, like the combat version, was to be worn above the left tunic pocket. It consisted of a three-inch-wide light blue enameled space (light blue being the infantry color) as background for an archaic rifle. The combat badge added an honorific "silver" wreath to this design and also added ten dollars to the wearer's monthly pay. It proved to no one's surprise that almost no soldier wanted to wear the expert badge, but that all wanted to add the combat version to their collection of decorations.

Broadly distributed, as it had to be, the CIB at least attested to the wearer's not running away in battle and having probably undergone an experience fairly hellish and thus knowing something adjacent to actual heroism, and the Combat Medic's Badge finally officially recognized what all combat soldiers knew, that the unarmed platoon medics were a lot braver than the armed troops, protected by nothing but red crosses on dirty armbands and helmets.

Because during the war the terrors and traumas occasioned by genuine infantry fighting could not be emphasized, lest soldiers' relatives be disheartened by the sad truth about the inevitability of ground-force casualties, the CIB seems never to have been sufficiently publicized and appreciated, but today some CIBs are still being worn among superannuated army people who "won" theirs in Korea or Vietnam.

What prestige the CIB had was sadly diminished after the Second World War when it was decided that a veteran owning one could also automatically be awarded the Bronze Star Medal, "for meritorious achievement in action against the enemy." But before that happened, the CIB, worn alone as if in contempt for ribboned "decorations," accrued a secret significant status.

One evening on Long Island, James Jones climbed willingly up to the attic to locate a box of war stuff his son had asked to see. As Willie Morris reports Jones saying while he sorted through the ribbons and their attachments,

> "This one here, it's the only one we wore when we shipped home." He pointed to the replica of a rifle on a field of blue with a silver wreath around it. "It's the Combat Infantryman's Badge."
>
> "Why," asks the boy, "why is that the only one you ever wore?"
>
> "Oh shit, I don't know. It was a point of pride, you see—better than all the rest. It spoke for itself. It really meant something. It was just an unbroken rule. If you wore any of the others, the men would've laughed you out of town, or maybe whipped your ass."

The difference is empirical. The badge was awarded for *being* in ultimate danger, the ribbons for what somebody *said* about your behavior—meaningless and probably corrupt testimony, as most infantrymen knew, having seen their battalion staffs piling up unearned honors. The CIB you earned without anyone "putting you in" for it. You knew, and the company roster knew, without anyone's agreement or ass-kissing, what you'd been through to wear it. It was private, almost secret, telling would-be melodramatists, "Don't ask." The CIB is the only thing pinned onto Robert Kotlowitz's jacket in the photo accompanying his memoir. The silence is eloquent, like the modesty it betokens.

There were other attempts to persuade the put-upon conscripts of the infantry that they were especially noble, even privileged. One notable try was composer Frank Loesser's song "Rodger Young," celebrating a heroic infantryman awarded the Medal of Honor posthumously for wiping out a Japanese machine-gun nest.

"Oh, they've got no time for glory in the infantry," Loesser's song began, prompting among skeptical listeners the silent comment, "Of course not. There isn't any." Loesser's song proved monumentally unsuccessful with both the troops and the folks at home, and Loesser, better known for the attractively cynical songs of *Guys and Dolls*, came clean once the war was over. As a composer at the mercy of the government, he declared, "You give [civilians] hope without facts: glory without blood. You give them a legend with the rough edges neatly trimmed."

As always, drink provided an antidote to fear and boredom, and here the troops in France were luckier than those in the Pacific, who had to manufacture their own liquor from potato skins and similar detritus. The discipline of the boys in France was constantly threatened by the alcohol problem, assisted by unguarded wine cellars and the availability of hitherto unknown drinks like Pernod as well as powerful liqueurs. Concerned about the morale of his outfit, one lieutenant suggested the usefulness of moderate doses of alcohol in getting his men through the worst days.

His fellow officers had all been killed or wounded and he was entirely in charge of a company. He had found a whole truckload of liquor left behind by the Germans, and with this he managed to keep his boys in a state of cheerful intoxication for days with Benedictine and champagne. They accounted for at least a thousand bottles, he reports, and "when some . . . showed signs of weakening and slowing up, I would give them four or five new bottles."

It is not widely known now, and was hardly known then, that the garrison liquor ration provided officers continued overseas. Even when dug in, officers found their two monthly bottles delivered directly to their foxholes. Memories differ, but one officer recalls being handed typically a quart of scotch and a pint of gin, plus two bottles of champagne and one of cognac—in case he wanted to mix up some French Seventy-Fives. Officers who did not drink—there were a few—sometimes called for squad leaders to come with canteen cups and receive donations for their boys.

Modes of Dishonor

Because the vast majority of the Boy Crusaders were unenthusiastic conscripts, their attitude toward the army and all its works was, in one degree or another, hostile. In combat they knew that there were only the three classic avenues of escape from the front line with its discipline, anxiety, and horror: the unlikely sudden end of the war; a wound; and death itself.

In intolerable situations, like weeks in the Hürtgen Forest, more men than usual decided simply to take off. If they had no idea of ever returning, their action was designated desertion, and the punishment was rumored to be, at worst, death by firing squad, or at least a long prison term in Fort Leavenworth or a similar tough place of confinement. In garrison, normally the related misdemeanor, absence without leave, was lightly punished unless the absence exceeded one month; then, it turned into desertion, stiffly punished but not so seriously as when committed in the face of the enemy.

In one episode in France a fresh battalion arrived on the line to relieve a unit battered by prolonged service there. The old unit had fought a serious action the day before, in which a number of men had been killed. Their bodies had not yet been removed, but were laid out neatly just behind the foxholes and decently covered with pine boughs. Among the relieving arrivals were two fresh new second lieutenants. When they saw these bodies, they instantly disappeared, to turn up many months later, profiting in the

Paris black market. As Kurt Vonnegut might be tempted to say, so it goes.

In Europe, there was more desertion than expected, and of course more than commonly publicized. Of the nineteen thousand or so acknowledged deserters from the American army, by 1948 only nine thousand had been captured. And for the English the situation was probably worse because home was closer. Journalist Pete Grafton heard a British soldier declare, "Almost every police station and detention camp in Britain was jam-packed full. . . . In Glasgow alone, deserters were sitting twelve to a cell." Many GIs were so scared that they required special attention. Says an American woman who worked with the Red Cross, "Just before they went across to France, belts and ties were removed from some of these young men. They were very, very young."

The motive for desertion at the front was usually, of course, unbearable fear. But sometimes it could be more complicated and subtle. Private Vernon Scannell was in the British and not the American infantry, but his desertion, like many others in both armies, was caused by something different from fright. In North Africa, he deserted, he says, not from cowardice (he was a tough prizefighter before the war) but disgust with his fellow soldiers when he witnessed them stealing watches, rings, and money from their dead mates' bodies. Questioned about his motives for leaving, he answered that "he walked away because of that hideous business of war," and denied that cowardice had anything to do with it. "What he had felt was a kind of hopeless disgust, disgust with his comrades who were looting the corpses, with the lunacy of war." What motivated him was, it would seem, something close to "taste."

Whatever the motive for running away, this action was

noted, obviously, in ground warfare, especially in places like France and Italy, where there was someplace to run away to. The motive doubtless existed in the navy and the air corps but the circumstances made it less likely. John Gregory Dunne, a U.S. Navy person, comments on the war he knew in the Pacific: "Out here the war life was all there was: no history was visible, no monuments of the past, no cities remembered from books. There was nothing here to remind a soldier of his other life: no towns, no bars, nowhere to go, nowhere even to desert to."

At any rate, there was a distinct difference between American and German reactions to the desertion impulse, which any soldier must have felt occasionally. In the American army, the idea of soldiers running away was considered as not unlikely: thus the institution in infantry platoons of the guide sergeant in the rear, whose duty (never discussed) was to catch and dissuade youngsters reacting to a powerful impulse to run to the rear. In the German army, such soldiers would be shot on sight. The difference is surely one of the things the war was about.

—

There was another expedient available to the absolutely terrified: a self-inflicted wound, not uncommon among frontline infantry when the going got very tough.

Probably no one knows exactly how many men shot their hands and feet, fingers and toes, to escape worse pain and horror. The relatively useless little finger was a favorite target. There's evidence that the number of such cases was large. One authority deposes that "men by the hundreds shot themselves in the foot or the hand to get out of the combat zone," in this case, the Hürtgen Forest. And the foot or hand was usually the left one, for, most boys being right-handed, the shooting had to be done with the right hand working with a pistol, carbine, or rifle. The brighter soldiers used some cloth—an empty sandbag would do—to avoid telltale powder burns near the bullet hole.

Hospitals saw so much of this desperate act that to save energy in record keeping, they devised its own abbreviation—SIW—and they established special wards for SIWs like the special wards for the victims of venereal disease, another form of self-inflicted wound, after all. When the SIW malefactor had recovered, in the absence of a witness to his act he was usually convicted of "carelessness with weapons" and sentenced to six months in the (peaceful) stockade—which of course was the aim of the whole thing. General Patton had seen his fill of the SIW act: in one hospital he found three curious cases of gunshot wounds, two men shot through the left leg, one through the left hand. "It is my experience," he wrote, "that anytime a soldier is shot through either of these extremities there is a high probability that the wound is self-inflicted." This was Patton's second world war and the "high probability" is that he knew what he was talking about.

One way of judging battalions and companies of infantry was their number of SIWs. SIWs were, together with battle-fatigue cases, administratively reported as "non-battle casualties," and as historian William O'Neill writes,

> The Army Research Branch used the ratio of non-battle to battle casualties as a measure of combat effectiveness, since it was axiomatic that companies with more non-battle casualties, usually self-inflicted, would send fewer men to the front. In actual practice it found that units with high rates of non-battle casualties were usually reluctant to go into battle and lacked self-confidence.

That's all very well, although it does err in assuming a large number of infantrymen avid to plunge into battle; it was an extremely painful duty for everyone, and even the best troops found it hard to conceal their fear. Ninety-nine percent would have escaped if there had been any non-shameful way out. It was only the buddy system, every soldier's audience of familiar moral acquaintances, that kept the boys, in this respect at least, honorable.

Treatment of Damaged Bodies, Alive and Dead

It should strike everyone as funny that armies at war are insane institutions devoted to two quite contradictory operations, both brought to the highest technological standard. One operation requires bringing death to people with the greatest efficiency. The other is rescuing people from death with the greatest efficiency. And those rescued are, crazily, not just members of the familiar, homegrown army but the despised enemy as well. In the Second World War, as soon as a soldier was wounded and removed to the hospital, he sloughed off the implications of his national identity and became merely another soldier "patient." There was, oddly, no longer the impulse to kill him but now the equally strong impulse to save him. Anyone in the hospital slipping him a dose of poison to hasten his demise could have been brought up on capital charges, charges all but unthinkable in the world just left behind of skillful, justified murder.

Professionals practicing military medicine are familiar with the analogous paradox articulated by Albert E. Cowdrey, an impressive historian of army medicine: "The war was not only a time when medicine and public health saved millions who otherwise would have been lost in the conflagration. It was the time also when the technology of destruction moved decisively ahead of the science of healing." An illustration of such technology might be the novel German antipersonnel mine, its height calculated to spray its metal parts nowhere but into the infantryman's irreparable testicles. Or one might evoke the easier example of the atom bomb.

The famous Geneva Convention (officially the Geneva Accords of 1929) guarantees these oddities, specifying the treatment of enemy wounded and prisoners, and the sanctity of medical aidmen in the field, as well as ambulances, hospitals, hospital ships, and other things marked by the Red Cross. According to the rules, medical aidmen must be entirely unarmed and identifiable by conspicuous red crosses. In World War II American aidmen (always "medics" to the troops) wore four red crosses painted on their helmets and a red cross armband on the left arm—and as they learned the facts of battlefield life, on the right arm as well. They were still underidentified in contrast to their German counterparts, who wore armbands and also a very visible white body tabard with large, two-foot-square red crosses on both front and back. Especially once they got dirty, the American red crosses were seldom visible enough in snow, rain, and dust storms, and then the only protection for the wounded was the shout, "Medic at work!" from the (as it were) sidelines.

When clearly seen the red cross on medics' clothing and hospital buildings and ambulances was generally respected by the German enemy, but in the battles against the Japanese (who had not signed the Geneva Accords), the red cross, as Albert Cowdrey says, tended to be "treated as a bull's-eye." (Before moving on, it might be worthwhile to glance at an idea of British captain John Tonkin, experienced in World War II. "I have always felt," he says, "that the Geneva Convention is a dangerous piece of stupidity, because it leads people to believe that war can be civilized. It can't.")

Each rifle platoon, where 85 percent of ground force casualties occurred, had one medic assigned as part of its required strength of forty boys. In the field he carried two capacious shoulder bags, one on each side, whose immense size could cause some fears for the future among sensitive troops. In these bags he carried his essential equipment for dealing with wounds and ailments: morphine Syrettes, to lessen pain and arrest shock; packets of sulfanilamide, for guarding against infection of wounds, always a danger considering the animal and human feces to be found on any battlefield; gauze bandages and large and small prepared compresses, with adhesive tape to keep them in place; ammonia capsules (for reviving the faint); tincture of Merthiolate for minor complaints like blisters, cuts, et cetera; aspirin; bismuth and paregoric, the standard remedy for diarrhea; scissors, to trim away clothing (and flesh) as needed and to cut the gauze; sodium amytal tablets, a mild sedative; and tags to attach to the wounded, indicating the time of morphine injection and other information useful to higher medical echelons. (The army Medical Department, fearing addiction, was extremely cautious about morphine, restricting it to small doses carefully timed and controlled.)

As a group, medics were found to be extraordinarily brave and dutiful, and many were religious, upon induction and training having asked to be assigned to some nonmurderous branch of the service. In combat, not to rush out of cover to treat a wounded boy would have severely damaged a medic's future usefulness to his platoon.

Being a medic was tough duty, both physically and morally. As Albert Cowdrey writes,

> Robert P. Phillips, an aidman serving with a rifle company of the 28th Division, found that heavy enemy artillery fire made him dread the cry of "Medic!" which forced him into the

open. Every wounded man had to be carried, dragged, or helped to shelter, and that meant moving slowly under fire. Shell fragments whittled down the trees and casualties increased; he remembered for the rest of his life the job of examining wounded men at night, cutting away clothes in the darkness, feeling for and discovering the wound ("It's like putting your hand in a bucket of wet liver."). Phillips himself was hit on September 25. He was bandaging a casualty when a shell fragment tore a hole in his own chest, mangling a dog-tag and sending him into the chain of evacuation along with his patient.

That chain, ideally, ran like this: It began with the medic's simple but difficult lifesaving treatment. Then, if the wounded boy couldn't walk and litters were available, he was conveyed by the two litter bearers (four was better) to the battalion aid station, some distance to the rear, where the tag applied by the medic was checked by a medical officer, and after further treatment, if needed, the patient was sent to a clearing station; after its attention, it in turn moved him to a field hospital or an evacuation hospital, the ultimate avenues to a general hospital. Each of these was equipped to do a certain amount and kind of surgery: for example, not every one had X rays for locating metal fragments. Finally, if not sent home because hopeless, the patient would recover at a convalescent hospital and then, if judged fully recovered, he would be sent, although scarred, back to a hated replacement depot, and then back to his unit, where the whole process would be likely to begin again.

In these various hospitals the surgeons, many in the army direct from civilian life with minimal military training, were startled to encounter challenges more taxing than hernia repair or appendectomies. Says Cowdrey: "The damage that weapons could inflict on the human body was varied and sometimes spectacular. Veterans remembered—and sometimes dreamed of, years after the war—bodies literally torn to pieces, of intestines hung on trees like Christmas festoons."

But the boys were menaced by something more than flying bits of metal. Beginning with the weather of late October, which grew cold and damp and promised to grow worse as real winter arrived, trench foot became the scourge of the foxholes. As General Bradley himself confessed, "When the rains came in November with a blast of wintry air, our troops were ill-prepared for winter-time campaigning." In September, expecting the war to end before freezing weather, Bradley "had deliberately by-passed shipments of winter clothing in favor of ammunition and gasoline." The result was the incapacitation of about 45,000 combat troops, the equivalent of the infantrymen of three divisions. And as winter proceeded to freeze the battlefields, the troops became aware of another instance of superior planning and achievement by the loathed enemy. In addition to German tanks and machine guns, the German aidman's body tabard was to be envied. And instead of carrying their wounded back on mere litters and slipping and sliding on snow and ice, the all-white-uniformed Krauts had nifty little sleds to fit the litters, and the whole setup could be pulled along by a rope with one hand, leaving the other free to wave a large Red Cross flag.

Something of what an American boy aidman might experience is recalled by T/5 Leo Litwak. A few months before, Litwak had been a student at the University of Michigan.

He was now, in the winter of 1944–45, an aidman in a rifle company fighting in the snow near the German border. As he says,

> I was an inexperienced nineteen-year-old kid. Only nineteen years old but I was called "Father" by a dying German soldier. We . . . were marching through a bleak, snow-drenched forest. . . . Two German soldiers struggled through the snow toward the trees, maybe two hundred yards away. The captain told Rebel to see if he could hit them. Rebel knelt, aimed, fired. One went down, the other made it into the woods. The downed man waved at us and the captain told me to go to him.
>
> The wounded German was no one to fear. I could see as we got close that he was an unlikely soldier, old and fragile, among the dregs the Germans were beginning to shove into combat. He must have been trying to surrender when we spotted him. He didn't have a weapon. He lay twisted around his right leg. He wore a gray wool uniform and cap, his eyes huge, his face pinched and unshaven, his mouth stretched as if shrieks were coming out, but it was a smothered sound, *Ohhhhh, Ohhhhh.* He saw the red crosses on my arms and helmet and reached for me and cried, *"Vater!"* Father. A spike of femoral bone was sticking through his trousers. I slit his pants, bared the wound at midthigh. He'd shit small, hard, gray turds—what you might see in the spoor of an animal. The shit had worked itself down near the fracture. The stink was pungent and gagging. I put sulfa powder on the exposed bone, covered it with a compress, tied a loose tourniquet above the wound high on the thigh. He was graying fast, going into shock. He said *"Vater, ich sterbe."* Father, I'm dying. I stuck morphine into his thigh. He wasn't eased and I gave him another eighth of a grain. I watched him lapse into shock—lips blue, sweat cold, skin gray, pupils distended, pulse weak and fluttery.

I felt as if I, too, had been shot. I yearned for him to be dead so we'd both be relieved from his pain.

The living are complicated but the dead have been stripped of all meaning.

We saw them coifed in crab-shaped helmets, dressed in gray uniforms, mouth agape, gray teeth, gray hands, worn boots, no identities, indistinguishable one from the other, dead meat, nothing to grieve.

We were stupefied by the death we'd breathed, and stumbled toward combat clutched by the fear that we, too, could be made simple.

Who attended to the dead old men, and the dead Germans and American students, once they became a rigid, stinking, unpitied nuisance? The morale and the innocence of the fighting troops would have been jeopardized if they themselves had had to pick up corpses they knew and carry them to burial places. Thus the work was done by anonymous noncombatant troops, members of the Graves Registration Details of the Quartermaster Corps. They were unlikely to have known any of those whose bodies they collected and so, if they were lucky, could do the heartbreaking work with little emotion. If any emotion did enter, it could be handled, as it was, with the help of alcohol, practically a necessity for this kind of work. Many of the bodies could be located only by smell, and most were days or weeks old and in what might be called poor condition. And they weren't laid out neatly, or even formed up into decent skirmish lines. One Quartermaster body collector, who had been busy in a major battle area, had this to say: "Everywhere we searched we found bodies, floating in the rivers, trampled on the roads, bloated in the ditches, rotting in the bunkers, pretzeled into foxholes, burned in the tanks, buried in the snow, sprawled in doorways, splattered in gutters, dismembered in mine fields, and even literally blown up into trees." American bodies tended to wear a set of two dogtags. One would be nailed to the top of the wooden stake marking the soldier's burial spot. The other would be retained for later checking if necessary.

The identification tag for German bodies was in two parts and handled the same way, only the body was not allowed a separate grave. Large pits were the Germans' communal resting places, merely sanitary rather than in any way funereal or commemorative. The German military cemeteries created well after the war feature not the emblems of individual graves but large mounds marking deep burial pits. Probably appropriate, in a way, given the National Socialist emphasis on group behavior and identity.

THE BULGE

A low and comic word, to be sure, suggestive of dieting and what used to be called women's foundation garments. But it's handier than something like the German Winter Salient, so we'll stay with it.

"Neither side gained anything of value in the terrible fight for the Hürtgen Forest. But the battle did help the Germans disguise the tremendous build-up they were making in the Eifel Mountains opposite France's Ardennes Forest." Thus says Donald L. Miller, who notes that in the fall of 1944, Eisenhower bet Montgomery five pounds that the war would be over by Christmas. That sort of optimism was widely shared in late November and December, and the Allied generals saw little danger in using the Ardennes as a place to rest overworked divisions and to acquaint newcomers, like the 106th Division, with some of the milder elements of infantry warfare like observing, patrolling, and supplying. Secure in the expectation that nothing was going to happen, the Americans employed only four divisions to defend the sixty-mile line, and these were spread very thinly. The Germans meanwhile rebuilt their assault strength to thirteen infantry and seven armored divisions, collecting some 250,000 troops to deal with the Americans' 83,000. Despite their many severe reverses up to this point, the Germans fielded two Panzer armies totalling 1,940 tanks, while the Americans considered themselves sufficiently provided with 400—and these were largely Shermans, which had already proved, with their thinner armor and liability to flame up, hardly a match against the German Tigers. But Christmas packages for the boys were arriving from home and that old, warm American optimism was comforting all ranks.

There were actually plenty of intelligence reports of strengthened German activity behind their line: heavy tank noise was heard and noted; spotter planes saw and brought back news of odd armored-vehicle concentrations hiding in forests. So the problem was not really paucity of evidence and data. It was, as so often, complacency and the lust for intellectual comfort overriding the meaning of evidence. The Americans' Ardennes intelligence failure takes its place in a long line of similar, apparently inexplicable modern events, like the failure of radar to convey that immense groups of Japanese planes were approaching Pearl Harbor. And an astonishing failure of inquiry and understanding dates from the Vietnam War, where observers were oddly slow to figure out how the Vietcong were able to penetrate the undamaged walls and fences surrounding a certain airport and plant explosives on planes. The answer to the mystery finally became clear: the unsuspectedly clever and indefatigable enemy had entered the American position not over or through the gates and walls and fences but from tunnels under the airport, whose openings at ground level provided access to the whole place. Given these numerous failures of the mind to detect what afterward seems almost obvious, one must conclude that the mind is not so capable as it pretends of producing trustworthy knowledge, so easily is it threatened by fatigue, pride, laziness, and selfish inattention.

His armies badly roughed up in Normandy and western France, as early as August 1944 Hitler sensed that the war in the West could not be won, and it seemed that in his army's weakened condition only a series of delaying defensive operations would be possible. But there was one slender bit of hope. During these defensive actions, he hoped the enemy coalition of capitalist West and Communist East would come apart, as, he persuaded himself, military coalitions always had—Italy's disinclination to continue alliance with Germany was an example. If an armistice with the West was to be achieved, it had to occur in a context of regained German power, and how was that to be brought about? If the war in the West concluded with some sort of agreement (Hitler never had an adequate idea of the Allies' hatred of the Reich and its cruel racial usages, which lay behind the Allies' unwavering insistence on unconditional surrender), Germany's full power could be applied to the eastern front and the Soviets could be held, driven back, or even conquered. Thus, at a meeting in September with senior officers, after delivering one of his tedious, wandering morale speeches, Hitler thought for a bit, and then blurted out: "I have made a momentous decision. I shall go over to the offensive, that is to say, out of the Ardennes, with the objective, Antwerp!" It was 125 miles away. Keitel's and Jodl's eyebrows ascended as they regarded each other with shock. They knew there was no way Germany could succeed with such an attack. She was short of manpower, airpower, fuel, steel, and weapons. But his fanciful plan, Hitler thought, could split British from American forces, leaving the Americans alone in the south and the British alone in the north. Then that coalition would come apart too and the whole shape and dynamics of the war in Europe would change. It was perhaps the mere word *Ardennes* that set him off on this wild notion, for it was through that heavily wooded area in 1940 that his unsuspected Panzers had swarmed into France and forced the French surrender in little more than three weeks.

His new plan envisaged two Panzer armies, the Sixth SS in the north and the Fifth in the south. Thirty-eight divisions were to be involved and almost one thousand planes were somehow to be accumulated. This time the Ardennes attack plan required more gasoline than what was on hand, so the hope was to capture gasoline from an Allied dump on the way. That was the sort of dubious detail senior Wehrmacht officers found impossible, and there were no officers who regarded the plan as anything but absurd, a formula simply for disaster, much too ambitious for successful execution.

For Hitler's Ardennes plan, absolute secrecy was crucial and every means was invoked—restricting information from all but a few, cutting off radio traffic, and even laying straw on the approach roads to soften the sound of tank treads and truck and cannon wheels. Because no one on the German side blabbed, the hour-and-a-half artillery barrage from almost two thousand guns at five-thirty on the morning of December 16 was a total surprise to the foxhole troops who received it. Among the recipients was the 28th Division, still shaken by the horrors of Hürtgen Forest, and the 106th Infantry Division, entirely unblooded—up to now.

It was dark and it was foggy when the boys, stomachs paralyzed by fear, first saw shapes moving silently toward them, and then, as the shapes advanced, they saw the white snow garments and unique helmets of the German infantry, psyched up to kill them all. In the ghastly weather, you either fought back a bit against the bayonet and the grenade or you took off. If you were wounded outdoors you froze to death within a half hour.

It would not be fair to depict what happened to the 106th Division as typical. The boys were young and they had been drafted and were not terribly well trained. Charles Whiting puts it bluntly: "There was no 'Crusade in Europe' for the young soldiers of the 106th Infantry Division." Those not immediately captured fled to the rear, many throwing away their weapons and howling, "The Krauts are coming." Those remaining on the line or close to it were hustled back east for long marches into prisoner-of-war cages. They were the eight thousand boys of two whole regiments of the 106th. Later narratives tried to brighten things up by noting that they said they were out of ammunition. This mass surrender was one of the most embarrassing moments in the history of the American military. Because an event like this was unthinkable, neither officers nor men were prepared for its ever happening. The army had barely noticed the training topic "Retrograde Movements," to employ the favored euphemism.

The British did it differently. At their battle schools, they used little playlets to show what might happen and to propose ways of meeting it. In one dramatization, the men refuse to follow their officer's order to follow him in an attack. They just lie there, looking at him with scorn. When he tries to animate them with shame and manly persuasion, they do nothing. As this crisis ripens, they lose patience and beat him up. When American soldiers encountered an experience somewhat like that, they had been allowed to imagine it would never happen. About the possibility of such situations arising, Fort Benning had been silent, and for the 106th, the result was an appalling rout.

The replacement and training systems bore some of the blame. Many of the soldiers who "bugged out" had been drafted and trained as if they were inert objects without human ideas or civilized subtleties leaking in. And in many battalion and regimental headquarters, there was similar panic, and not a few majors and colonels took off for the rear under various pretexts: "I must go see about ammunition," "I must go make sure our left flank is fastened down," and so on. Officers' arms and equipment were thrown away, just like the boys'. Documents were burned without orders, and commands to stand fast were "not heard," or even issued, and there was lying wherever it seemed the best course. There was quite a bit of intramural abuse and insult. One officer was heard to shout at a colonel, "Why, you're a goddamn coward!"

Normally, in the ground combat forces, it is assumed that orders are given in good faith and that they will be obeyed: that officers will, of course, share the risks of the men, that unit cohesion and the chain of command will be honored, that the vertical element of ranks will continue to sustain meaning and cohesion.

But the Ardennes disaster became a rare theater of disgrace, an exposé of military affectations of competence and courage.

With the Americans in disorder, it was not possible for Montgomery to ignore the opportunity to seize power. On December 19 he telegraphed General Sir Alan Brooke, the British Imperial Chief of Staff, and said, "The situation in the American area is not repeat not good. . . . Great confusion and all signs of a full-scale withdrawal. There is a definite lack of grip and control and no one has a clear picture as to situation. . . . Ike ought to place me in operational command of all troops on the northern half of the front."

Ike did, to the deep annoyance of generals Bradley and Patton. Monty's temporary command of both American and British troops on the northern front of the Bulge provided him with materials for one of his worst breaches of taste and tact. In a large press conference he exhibited the self-praise and contempt for his American ally that he had shown before, but not to so large an audience.

But all changed on the twenty-third of December. The weather cleared and the American air corps went into action. From then on, the Allied cause was more secure, additional divisions being called in to bolster the renewed attack. But driving the Germans back to their initial positions was a ghastly, monthlong operation. As Donald L. Miller notes, "That month was a horror for American troops. In January, 1945, the U.S. Army suffered more battle casualties—over 39,000—than in any other month in the fight for northwest Europe." Because it was cleaning up an unforgivable mess instead of taking new territory and destroying new opposition, the details were not so well publicized. But the ruinous old horrors were still going on. Of the fighting in this month, an infantryman says, "People didn't crumble and fall like they did in the Hollywood movies. They were tossed in the air and their blood splattered everywhere. And a lot of people found themselves covered in the blood and flesh of their friends, and that's a pretty tough thing for anybody to handle," especially a teenage boy replacement who once thought himself safe in the ASTP. Another young infantryman tells of being in a foxhole with a buddy in late December:

> Gordon got ripped by a machine gun from roughly the left thigh through the right waist. He . . . told me he was hit through the stomach as well. . . . We were cut off. . . . We

were in foxholes by ourselves, so we both knew he was going to die.

We had no morphine. We couldn't ease [the pain] so I tried to knock him out. I took off his helmet, held his jaw up, and just whacked it hard as I could, because he wanted to be put out. That didn't work so I hit him up by the head with a helmet and that didn't work. Nothing worked. He slowly froze to death, he bled to death.

As a reminder of the spirit of the American infantry, it's a pity that scene has not attained the familiarity of the one featuring the rejoinder "Nuts!"

The final reckoning of the American Bulge casualties:

Dead boys:	19,000
Wounded boys:	48,000
"Missing" (mostly prisoners):	21,000

German troop casualties are not known, although about 110,000 became prisoners and 1,400 of their tanks were lost.

The Skorzeny Affair

Back in October, many weeks before the Bulge attack, Field Marshal Keitel sent to selected Wehrmacht units this message, not by radio but by safer teleprinter:

> VERY SECRET. To divisions and army commands only. Officers and men who speak English are wanted for a special mission. The Führer has ordered the formation of a special unit of approximately two battalion strength for use on the Western Front in special operations and reconnaissance. Volunteers who are selected will report to Dienstelle Skorzeny at Friedenthal.

(That is, the Skorzeny Company Office, as if some commercial firm were meant. Lieutenant Colonel Otto Skorzeny had impressed Hitler by skillfully managing the liberation of Mussolini from his place of banishment in the Italian mountains.)

A number of volunteers responded to Keitel's message, and 150 men were chosen for this special unit, designated Panzer Brigade 150. They were given a language test to determine their mastery of English, with emphasis on American idiom and pronunciation. As their D day approached, these German soldiers were formed into nine four-man teams dressed in American uniforms and riding in captured American jeeps and similar frontline vehicles. Their mission was to cross secretly to the American side and cause as much confusion and trouble as possible, cutting telephone lines, providing wrong directions at crossroads, and planting demoralizing rumors. They were equipped with suicide capsules to use if captured and trained to resemble GIs in every possible way, including slouching postures, gum chewing, leaning against walls when tired, keeping hands in trouser pockets, and when appropriate (all the time?) uttering American profanity and obscenity with heavy stress on the word *shit.*

Those GI impersonators who feared they might be in espionage trouble were reassured that their behavior was safely within the traditions of ground warfare. When one uncertain officer asked General Jodl if this venture was fully protected by international law, he was told that this was simply a *ruse de guerre,* or war stratagem, the sort of thing the Americans had already practiced widely, and they had also bombed women and children, so all was perfectly acceptable. He knew it was not, but saying so might have jeopardized the operation and risked unacceptable damage to the already struggling Third Reich.

So Skorzeny's jeep teams advanced confidently into the American area and did what damage they could. One bogus GI, wearing an MP's helmet, managed at a crossroads to misdirect a whole regiment rushing to bolster defense at the front. But as news of these deceptions rapidly spread, the Americans began applying test questions to GIs who looked inauthentic or acted suspiciously. (For one thing, GIs seldom rode four in a jeep.) The test questions have produced a comic collection of pop-culture materials, like "What's the name of the Brooklyn baseball team?" and "Where does 'Lil Abner' live?" These were useful to U.S. public relations in adding a dimension of the charming and the funny to episodes only bloody and horrifying. The same with the melodrama attending most accounts of the presumed threat to Eisenhower's safety, way back in Versailles, posed by these phony GIs. Often the passage of the false jeeps was blocked by MPs searching for deserting American troops or officers who were hustling for the rear "to check with battalion," or similar fraudulent errands.

Not many boys killed in the war had their names published and news of the details of their death and its setting spread abroad before the war was over. Not so with Gunther Billing, Wilhelm Schmidt, and Manfred Pernass, three of Skorzeny's people who were executed as spies by a firing squad. A news photograph of their being fastened to tall posts and then drooping in death appeared widely, presumably to convey an image of the seriousness of the war, the skill of American counterintelligence, and an implicit notice to the Germans that their cute trick wasn't working as well as they had hoped.

And there were more telling ways to catch Skorzeny's men than facetious questioning. Every American officer carried, in addition to the metal identity tags around his neck, a laminated card with his photo. These cards had one curious feature: an uncorrected typographical error. The top of the card read NOT A PASS. FOR INDENTIFICATION ONLY. Someone preparing the disguises of the Skorzeny spies couldn't resist—some will say "in a German manner"—pedantically correcting the spelling on the false cards issued to those masquerading as American officers. (It would probably be too much to regard the error as intentional, committed for anticounterfeiting purposes: it was too noticeable.)

The Peiper Affair

The momentary success of the German Ardennes counteroffensive had caused extensive civilian panic and mass hysteria in Belgium and Luxembourg. Some German tanks had penetrated thirty miles into what had recently been Allied territory. Fearing complete reversal of the war, some civilians pulled down the Stars and Stripes and replaced them with swastikas, and those who had done favors for the Allies especially feared the return of the Gestapo and its punishments.

That was the general situation when Waffen SS *Obersturmbannführer* (Lieutenant Colonel) Joachim Peiper was involved in trouble near the town of Malmédy. The so-called Malmédy Massacre, for which he was blamed, haunted him for the rest of his life. He was leading his tanks, almost out of fuel, toward the famous rumored American gasoline and oil dump when he encountered on the same road the trucks of an American battalion. He engaged them with machine-gun fire, which caused the GIs who were not instant casualties to flee into an adjoining field.

"The GIs had been told not to surrender to the enemy's armored groups," writes Donald L. Miller. "If they had to surrender, they should do so only to infantry units. These had the manpower to take Americans back as prisoners of war; the panzer units did not." One experienced GI articulated the rule: "Fight to the death or run like hell, but don't surrender." But these Americans had no choice. Perceiving that they were hopelessly outnumbered and faced by SS tanks, they stopped running and raised their empty hands in surrender—to be cut down by multiple machine guns. Eighty-six American soldiers died there; twenty or so managed to escape into nearby woods.

As commander of the SS unit, Peiper bore the blame, but actually he wasn't there at the moment of this massacre. He had gone up the road to capture an American general rumored to have his headquarters in a nearby town, and disappointed there, he returned to his own men to find the deed done. At the postwar trial of those who had done the shooting, it was shown that Peiper had trained them to be tough, if not exactly murderers of unarmed boys. He was sentenced to death, but in the new Cold War atmosphere of leniency toward the Germans, he was paroled after eleven years of imprisonment. His later life was darkened by threats of revenge from some French people with long memories, and his death in 1976 was bizarre. (See page 161.)

THE END

Driving the enemy back to his original jump-off line in the Ardennes by the end of January, American troops continued their postponed attacks eastward, and it seemed that many Germans, especially those in Waffen SS units, fought more "fanatically" as they were forced back onto the sacred soil of the Reich. Despite their catastrophic losses in the Bulge—an estimated nineteen thousand killed—the Americans still had almost three million men in forty-nine divisions, and weather permitting, their tactical employment of fighter-bombers remained an important element of their undoubted superiority over the Germans.

Many significant rivers had stood in the way of the Americans' rush to Germany. They had dealt with the Seine and the Saar and the Ruhr, but the Rhine remained, presenting the hardest challenge both because of its width and its importance to enemy morale. In German folklore it constituted a sort of sacred western border, and its violation by the Allies would suggest that total defeat was looming. As the Allies approached, the Germans knew that the many Rhine bridges would have to be destroyed, but timing was crucial: the bridges must not be destroyed until the last German troops had used them in their escape to the east bank. All the bridges had been satisfactorily blown up by German engineers—except one, the large, heavy Ludendorff railway bridge at Remagen, a town some twenty-five miles south of Cologne. On March 7, as twenty-two

American infantry and armored divisions approached, at the last moment the Wehrmacht captain responsible for the demolition set off the crucial charges, but many of them didn't go off, the wires apparently having been cut by the American artillery. The few explosions did send some lumber and debris into the air, but the bridge still stood and the Americans reached it. The news that they had captured an important bridge excited the American leadership into rapid action and a change of attack plans, and at Eisenhower's command, five divisions rushed over the bridge before the Germans could destroy it with artillery and aerial bombing, and even with swimmers trying to install new explosives. After ten days, the bridge finally collapsed, killing twenty-eight American engineers. By this time, the bridge having been fully exploited, fifty-seven American pontoon bridges crossed the river, many sporting signs like

CROSS THE RHINE WITH DRY FEET
Courtesy of the Ninth Armored Division

The German captain responsible for this fiasco was of course immediately sentenced to death by Hitler, but before he could be shot, he became a happy prisoner of war.

As the war neared its end, there were still bellicose actions from the enemy: lunatic shootings from stubborn SS youngsters, attacks on tanks by the pitiable *Volksturm* elderly wielding *Panzerfausts.* But some lucky American units now found themselves eliminating amateur roadblocks and collecting willing prisoners, or watching villagers display white cloths to indicate that their town was surrendering and that no German troops were to be found there.

As the Americans continued their attacks, the problem

of accommodating the hundreds of thousands of prisoners became acute, and many were collected outdoors in frigid areas surrounded by a few strands of barbed wire. Certainly unhealthy and unpleasant, but better than being killed. Further Rhine crossings took place during March, with many U.S. troops ferried over in landing craft manned by American sailors, imported across Europe for this task. By April 11, the American boys arrived at Magdeburg on the Elbe River, and on April 25 at Torgau, on the Elbe, they met, shook hands, wept, and danced with the Russians, signaling the positive end of the European war and the undeniable death of Hitler's Germany.

But in early April a shocking Nazi horror had been revealed.

The Camps

General Bradley had heard something startling from a credible German deserter that he thought worth investigating. It was news of a nearby underground communication center constructed by slave workers from the labor camp Ohrdruf-Nord, just south of the nearby town of Gotha. Patton's troops set out to investigate. On April 4 they found Ohrdruf, the first of the slave labor camps destined to horrify what remained of the civilized world.

Here a distinction must be made between slave labor camps like Ohrdruf, Dachau, Nordhausen, and Buchenwald, soon to be discovered, and such industrialized killing institutions as Auschwitz-Birkenau. The slave labor camps were in Germany proper, and their function was to provide workers, no matter how badly treated, for crucial industries located nearby, like I. G. Farben Chemicals, Siemens Electric, and Bayer Pharmaceutical.

The function of the other kind of camps was quite different. They were not in Germany but all in Poland, as if their operations were admittedly too nasty to be associated with high German purpose, that is, eugenics, which by killing off Jews and other undesirables, especially in the border area of Russia, could make room for German settlements there and elsewhere in "the East." In short, the function of the death camps was to forward the Final Solution of the Jewish problem, as set forth at the infamous Wannsee Conference in January 1942. The five large killing institutions in Poland operated by subjecting to Zyklon B gas the men, women, and children from all over Europe left alive who would increase the Jewish population, and most were killed in due course instantly on their arrival by rail. A few were selected from each train to help run the camp: they were killed in a short time.

Not that the slave labor camps didn't perform on occasion a similar function, as long as it did not interfere with industrial production and the work schedule. In these camps those few Jews found to be nonproductive, "worthless mouths" were satisfactorily carried off by cholera, tuberculosis, typhus, and starvation. These, together with shooting, were the main causes of the naked, open-eyed, open-mouthed, emaciated, stinking corpses Patton's boys found at Ohrdruf in fifty cattle cars and "dormitories," and strewn outdoors everywhere. Many had been shot the night before the Americans arrived.

General Bradley remembered the horror of this discovery:

> More than 3,200 naked emaciated bodies had been flung into shallow graves. Others lay in the streets where they had fallen. Lice crawled over the yellow skin of their sharp, bony frames. . . . The blood had congealed in coarse black scabs where the starving prisoners had torn out the entrails of the dead for food. . . . I was too revolted to speak. For here death had been so fouled by degradation that it both stunned and numbed us.

General Eisenhower was soon informed of the discovery, and so was Churchill. After seeing the spectacle for himself, Eisenhower ordered American legislators as well as nearby German civilians to visit, and demanded that the decent burial of all this horror was to be undertaken by the local civilians, who denied knowledge of anything that had taken place at their nearby institution. The mayor of neighboring Gotha and his wife went home and hanged themselves, whether in attempted expiation of the crime or fear of Allied punishment is not known. Hearing of this apparent evidence of guilt and shame, Eisenhower said, "Maybe there is hope after all."

Many who came to see the camp found all this so sickening that they simply threw up. They included tough journalist Bill Walton of *Time* magazine, as well as Lieutenant Colonel Walter J. Fellenz, who, while inspecting "a storage warehouse" containing over four thousand starved dead bodies, "vomited three times," he said, "in less than five minutes." Those of his troops who thought Patton appropriately characterized as "ol' blood and guts" would have been surprised and perhaps instructed to know that at Ohrdruf, the sight and the stench caused him, almost alone of the inspecting generals, to withdraw behind the corner of a building and throw up.

As visitors accumulated to view the horrors, local guides sprang up among surviving inmates. One self-appointed explainer of the workings of the camp was asked by Eisenhower why, if he had been a prisoner, he looked so well nourished. His answer is not recorded, but some of the prisoners provided the answer when they killed him as soon as they could.

There were many similar acts of turncoat moral obtuseness, suggesting that most Nazis saw nothing wrong with the system. When the British captured the camp at Belsen, the commandant, Josef Kramer, apparently didn't notice, or care, that in his speeches celebrating the efficiency of the establishment and noting his own contribution to its distinction, every sentence was providing evidence toward his own indictment, trial, and hanging. That sort of insensitivity about what strangers might think of the Third Reich's inhuman proceedings is comparable to Heinrich Himmler's assumption after his capture that if he could only meet with Eisenhower and persuade him that the Americans should now join the Wehrmacht, what was left of it, and turn against the Russians to save the world from the curse of Jewish Bolshevism, all could be saved. It was at about the time he was certain that line of persuasion wouldn't work that he bit his cyanide capsule and died instantly. But he had tried.

When the camp at Dachau was entered by the American boys, the U.S. Army motion picture photographer Walter Rosenblum was filming the whole thing. He says, "Some of the American troops were so upset by what the Nazis had done that they shot some of the German guards." As Donald L. Miller reports,

> A U.S. Army squad guarding about 122 SS prisoners, who continued swearing threats at their former prisoners, opened fire with machine guns and killed all of them.
>
> At that point the soldiers turned over the remaining guards to the inmates. One GI gave an inmate a bayonet and watched him behead a guard. Many of the guards were shot in the legs and could not move. A number of these disabled guards were ripped apart limb from limb.

Rosenblum later presented his film to his signal corps unit for processing and circulation. Nothing happened. The film was not shown at the war-crimes trials of the SS, because, Rosenblum speculates, in a strict sense it incriminated the boys who shot on behalf of the Dachau inmates, who had their own heyday of just revenge. Martha Gellhorn reported that "behind one pile of dead [inmates] lay the clothed healthy bodies of the German guards who had been found in this camp. They were killed at once by the prisoners when the American army entered."

These informal acts of justice, if it be that, were now echoed when possible among the ground troops still fighting. Said a company commander in a tank battalion, "We had just mopped them up before, but we stomped the shit out of them after the camps." A lieutenant who helped liberate Dachau declared, "I will never take another German prisoner armed or unarmed. How can they expect to do what they have done and simply say, 'I quit,' and go scot free? They are not fit to live." A soldier from New Zealand ratified the troops' conclusion when he said of the Germans, "They're not human at all"—ironically, the same words the Nazis used as they put to death countless "subhuman" Poles and Russians.

For the boys who fought, the first four months of 1945 were special. For one thing, there was a sense that the war would probably be over by the spring and that it would be foolish to be killed or maimed so near the end. The boys displayed more signs of combat caution than earlier and became harder to lead into hazardous action—by commanders who actually felt the same as the troops.

Also there was this heightened contempt for the Germans, both military and civilian, the result of rumors of the Malmédy Massacre and the stomach-turning facts of the camps. Formerly, it had been possible to treat a captured young, scared German soldier like a sad, put-upon conscript—that is, if he didn't prolong his firing immoderately or kill some admired member of the assault team. Now, however, Germans who surrendered were treated like SS monsters, kicked and beaten upon capture and often murdered on the way back from the line. A prisoner was treated with special severity if he was wearing any item of U.S. Army issue, which could be imagined stolen from a dead Yank.

The ill treatment of surrendering German soldiers was especially poignant if a soldier, approaching Americans with hands raised, held in one a bit of printed orange paper headed *Passierschein* ("safe conduct"). Millions of these were dropped by Allied aircraft in the last days of the war. Everything about them was designed to look "official" and valuable. They were headed by British and American coats of arms and used various "banknote" typographical and ornamental devices making them look like priceless certificates. Their designers clearly hoped to exploit the German soldiers' presumed respect for anything "official," especially if it expressed the will of a higher commander. The text of the *Passierschein,* in both German and English, was masterly in the way it promised everything desired by the poor prisoner, except a good, stiff drink:

> SAFE CONDUCT
>
> The German soldier who carries this safe conduct is using it as a sign of his genuine wish to give himself up. He is to be disarmed, to be well looked after, to receive food and medical attention as required, and to be removed from the danger zone as soon as possible.

This was followed by the facsimile signature of Dwight D. Eisenhower, Supreme Commander, Allied Expeditionary Force. American soldiers who solemnly collected these from surrendering German soldiers added verisimilitude by acting as if without a *Passierschein* a surrender was not legal, and threatening to send the men back whence they came, a punishment far surpassing a kicking or beating.

As the war ignominiously petered out, the troops knew more about the enemy than they had known when, early on, they had sneered or giggled at the word *crusade.* They had seen and smelled the death camps, and now they were able to realize that all along they had been engaged in something more than a mere negative destruction of German military power. They had been fighting and suffering for something positive, the sacredness of life itself.

Hardly any boy infantryman started his career as a moralist, but after the camps, a moral attitude was rampant and there was no disagreement on the main point. In the last few weeks of the war close to five thousand labor camps and prisons were discovered, most filled with unspeakable evidence of wanton cruelty. J. Glenn Gray, of the counterintelligence corps, wrote, "There may be a real purpose in it all, which is perceived only at the end of the journey. Somehow I feel that is true." Major Richard Winters said after seeing the corpses at the camp at Landsberg: "Now I know why I am here."

Officers and men agreed on this one thing. General James M. Gavin, commanding the 82nd Airborne Division, wrote:

> We had left in our wake thousands of white crosses from Africa to Berlin. And when it came to an end, there was not a man in the ranks of the 82nd Airborne Division who did not believe it was a war that had to be fought.... It had been a long and costly journey, and when we overran the concentration camps and looked back with a better understanding of where we had been, we knew it had been a journey worth every step of the way.

The boys' explosive little tour in France had been a crusade after all.

Martha Gellhorn happened to be at Dachau at the moment Germany surrendered unconditionally, and that seemed a most significant coincidence. She wrote: "For surely this war was made to abolish Dachau and all the other places like Dachau and everything that Dachau stands for. . . . We are not entirely guiltless, we the Allies, because it took us twelve years to open the gates of Dachau. We were blind and unbelieving and slow, and that we can never be again."

SERIOUSNESS

Today, after all the chatter about the Good War and the suggestions of special virtue among the boyish citizen soldiers, it is not easy to remember our view of the European enemy before the Cold War's requirement that the German military be resuscitated to the appearance of decency and, now no longer the Wehrmacht but the Bundeswehr, be rearmed, retrained, and prepared to oppose the new bugbear, the Russians. It is not easy to recall that when the war ended, the Germans, large and small, civilian and military, were despised as loathsome sadists who by their behavior, their laws, and their extermination camps had earned widespread contempt and deserved serious punishment.

It is hardly surprising that many Europeans, their countries ruined, take the war more seriously than Americans and nurse hatreds sure to take a long time wearing off. Some French citizens living in the country near ex–SS colonel Peiper, blamed for the infamous shooting of unarmed American prisoners as well as many Belgian civilians, waited thirty-two years to give their hatred full expression. Because war-crime courts had freed Peiper early, in 1976 his French neighbors got together and firebombed his house, making sure that he, but not his wife and children, was at home. When it was all over and his blackened body was found, it had shrunk to a length of sixty centimeters (two feet). The former scourge of Belgium and Luxembourg looked like a fireplace log past its best days. His murderers, who were delighted with that fact, have never been prosecuted.

Dwight Eisenhower was certainly a humane person, and that is one reason the troops, passing over the noisy and vulgar Patton, admired him and considered him practically the only American officer of high rank they would follow with pleasure. He had been brought up in Abilene's civilized church atmosphere and he was thoroughly indoctrinated there in the Golden Rule and related simple moral tenets.

His relative benignity suffered numerous blows during the war as he discovered more and more reasons to despise the Germans, not just the civilian Nazis but the army, deeply corrupted by National Socialist doctrine. In its Russian campaign, the regular German army assisted Himmler's SS commandos in murdering unarmed "Bolsheviks" and commissars, all in obedience to the Nazi insistence that this war was special because severely ideological, racial, and total: Jews and Russians must be not merely defeated but wiped out, lest their poison corrupt the whole world. Thus, when the German army was in Lithuania, photographs reveal that a mad, indeed fanatic local Nazi in the city of Kaunas assembled in a town square people he thought unfit to live and energetically beat them all to death with an iron bar until the square literally flowed with blood. On the outside of the wildly anti-Semitic crowd enjoying this spectacle stood troops of the Wehrmacht, not the SS as might be expected, smiling and laughing in their satisfaction at what they were beholding.

As even today more once-secret German documents are unearthed, the energy of the regular German army in its frequent forays against Jews and other "undesirables," and its cooperation with SS behavior, have become clear.

The deepened Nazification of the army was especially notable after the attempt on Hitler's life on July 20, 1944. After that event and its revelation of the number and quality of officers involved, the normal military salute was forbidden, to be replaced by the "Heil Hitler" Nazi substitute. In addition, Hitler discovered that the whole army was insufficiently National Socialized; he required to be installed in every company or similar military group a political officer whose lectures and counseling would remind each soldier and officer of his ideological as well as military duty.

Despite his boyish American decency, Eisenhower became a brutal and caustic critic of official Germany's moral status. One significant moment, not as well known as it should be, was on July 10, 1944. It took place at a lunch meeting with Lord Halifax, British ambassador to the United States; General Walter Bedell Smith and Harry C. Butcher were also there. Ike repeated his well-known views on the German general staff and his hopes for their future. As Butcher reports, "He would exterminate all of the General Staff." On second thought, he allowed that all of them might be permanently exiled like Napoléon to some "appropriate St. Helena," and never allowed to mix with civilized society again. Asked how many officers were on the general staff, "Ike guessed about 3,500." And, Butcher recalled, "He added that he would include for liquidation leaders of the Nazi party from mayors on up and all members of the Gestapo." *Extermination* and *liquidation* are serious words, and Ike is using them literally and seriously. He means, kill them all. Issues like that are what the war was about, our desire to pretend it couldn't have been notwithstanding.

And when he said those things, Eisenhower hadn't yet

seen the slave labor camps, especially Ohrdruf and Dachau. That awful experience simply underlined and validated his views about Germany. When it came time to accept the German surrender at Rheims, he indicated his unwillingness even to appear in the same room with the German signers and sent in his assistant Bedell Smith to do the job. His point: the Germans were not soldiers in the normal sense of the word. They were simply criminals and murdering trash, more fit for hanging than a handshake. After the signing he did condescend to address General Jodl, giving him minimal attention but making sure that he understood the terms of the surrender, presumably to prevent Jodl's later acting the swine and arguing some mistake. Extermination and liquidation would have to wait for the Nuremberg trials. There are some touching letters from Mrs. Jodl to Eisenhower, begging him to let her husband be executed by firing squad, traditionally a soldier's due. But Eisenhower denied these requests, knowing that Jodl faced the punishment not of a soldier but of a murderer, and he was properly hanged.

During their infantry preparation, American troops had been trained in killing with the bayonet. As in the First World War, such training involved the presumed development of personal hatred of the enemy—and his torso, head, and crotch. But the boys never took to this training very well. They seemed too good-natured to imagine themselves such vicious killers, and bayonet drill sometimes left them weak with laughter. It seemed they did not enjoy even simulating hatred, and they thought the whole thing rather comic. In 1942, when Eisenhower was trying to talk official Washington into some idea of what real war was like, he said, "The actual fact is that not one man in twenty in the government . . . realizes what a grisly, tough dirty business we are in." That certainly included also the infantry conscripts. The war over, in his Guildhall Address, Ike said of the Yanks who crowded into England preparing for the invasion, "Most were mentally unprepared for the realities of war—especially as waged by the Nazis." The absence in American troops of an appropriate hate of the enemy always bothered Eisenhower; he knew that plenty of hatred was aimed at the Japanese, who had directly attacked Americans on their own "soil," but that American soldiers weren't prepared to cultivate similar feelings toward the Germans, who had done them no great physical harm. Leaving Ohrdruf, Ike asked one GI, "Still having trouble hating them?" The answer the GIs would give him now was "No, sir!"

In August 1944, Private David Webster, who had fought the Germans and knew now what the war was, wrote home to his gentle, civilized parents:

> I cannot understand why you hope for a quick end of the war. Unless we take the horror of battle to Germany itself, unless we fight in their villages, blowing up their houses, smashing open their wine cellars, killing some of their livestock for food, unless we litter their streets with horribly rotten German corpses as was done in France, the Germans will prepare for war, unmindful of its horrors. Defeat must be brought into Germany itself before this mess can come to a proper end. . . .

Nasty as that may be, Eisenhower would say that there's a young man who has learned the right lesson. The years proved it unnecessary, but at the time it made a kind of sense available only to a boy who had enacted the role of a murderous Crusader and by some miracle survived.

Sources

Ambrose, Stephen E., *Citizen Soldiers.* New York, 1997.
Amis, Kingsley, *Memoirs.* London, 1991.

Barrette, George, quoted by Ralph G. Martin, *The GI War, 1941–1945.* Boston, 1945.
Belsey, James and Helen Reid, *West at War.* Bristol, 1990.
Blumenson, Martin, *Breakout and Pursuit.* Washington, DC, 1984.
Blunt, Roscoe C., *Foot Soldier: A Combat Infantryman's War in Europe.* Cambridge, MA, 1994.
Bradley, Omar N. and Clay Blair, *A General's Life.* New York, 1983.
Brett-James, Antony, *Conversations with Montgomery.* London, 1984.
Butcher, Harry C., Capt., USNR, *My Three Years with Eisenhower.* New York, 1946.

Carafano, James Jay, *After D-Day: Operation Cobra and the Normandy Breakout.* Boulder, CO, 2000.
Carell, Paul, *Invasion! They're Coming!* Atglen, PA, 1995.
Cole, H. M., *The Lorraine Campaign.* Washington, DC, 1950.
Coolrick, William K., Ogden Tanner et al., *The Battle of the Bulge.* New York, 1979.

Cowdrey, Albert E., *Fighting for Life: American Military Medicine in World War II.* New York, 1994.

Doubler, Michael D., *Closing with the Enemy: How GIs Fought the War in Europe, 1944–1945.* Lawrence, KS, 1994.

Dunne, John Gregory, "The Hardest War," *New York Review of Books,* Dec. 20, 2001, pp. 50 ff.

Egger, Bruce E. and Lee Macmillan Otts, *G Company's War.* Tuscaloosa, AL, 1992.

Eisenhower, David, *Eisenhower: At War, 1943–1945.* New York, 1986.

Eisenhower, Dwight D., *Crusade in Europe.* New York, 1948.

Eksteins, Modris, *Walking Since Daybreak.* New York, 1999.

Ellis, John, *One Day in a Very Long War.* London, 1998.

Featherston, Alwyn, *Battle for Mortain.* Novato, CA, 1998.

Felix, Charles Reis, *Crossing the Sauer: A Memoir of World War II.* Short Hills, NJ, 2002.

Fussell, Paul, *Wartime: Understanding and Behavior in the Second World War.* New York, 1989.

Gellhorn, Martha, *The Face of War.* New York, 1998.

Gilbert, Sir Martin, *The Second World War: A Complete History.* New York, 1989.

Grafton, Pete, *You, You, and You: The People out of Step with World War II.* London, 1981.

Hale, Edwin R. W. and Frayn Turner, *The Yanks Are Coming.* New York, 1983.

Hart, S. et al, *The German Soldier in World War II.* Osceola, WI, 2000.

Hastings, Max, *Overlord: D-Day and the Battle for Normandy.* New York, 1984.

Huie, William Bradford, *The Execution of Private Slovik.* New York, 1954.

Jones, James, *WWII.* New York, 1975.

Keegan, Sir John, *The Battle for History: Re-Fighting World War II.* Toronto, 1995.

———, *Six Armies in Normandy: From D-Day to the Liberation of Paris.* New York, 1982.

Klemperer, Victor, *The Language of the Third Reich: A Philologist's Notebook,* trans. Martin Brady. New Brunswick, NJ, 2000.

Knox, Bernard, quoted by Roger Spiller in "My Guns."

Kotlowitz, Robert, *Before Their Time.* New York, 1997.

Litwak, Leo, *The Medic: Life and Death in the Last Days of WWII.* Chapel Hill, NC, 2002.

Loesser, Frank, quoted by Richard R. Lingeman, *Don't You Know There's a War On?: The American Home Front, 1941–1945.* New York, 1970.

Longmate, Norman, *The GI's: The Americans in Britain, 1942–1945.* London, 1975.

MacDonald, Charles B., *The Battle of the Huertgen Forest.* Philadelphia, 1963.

———, *The Siegfried Line Campaign.* Washington, DC, 1963.

McKee, Alexander, *Caen: Anvil of Victory.* New York, 1984.

McLogan, Russell E., *Boy Soldier: Coming of Age During World War II.* Reading, MI, 1998.

Macksey, Kenneth, *Why the Germans Lose at War: The Myth of German Military Superiority.* London, 1996.

Marshall, S. L. A., *Bringing Up the Rear: A Memoir.* San Francisco, 1979.

Miller, Donald L. and Henry Steele Commager, *The Story of World War II.* New York, 2001.

Morris, Willie, *James Jones: A Friendship.* New York, 1978.

O'Neill, William L., *A Democracy at War: America's Fight at Home and Abroad in World War II.* New York, 1993.

Orwell, George, *The Collected Essays, Journalism, and Letters of George Orwell,* eds. Sonia Orwell and Ian Angus. 4 vols. New York, 1968.

Patton, George S., *War as I Knew It.* New York, 1947.

Perret, Geoffrey, *There's a War to Be Won: The United States Army in World War II.* New York, 1991.

Pulver, Murray, quoted by Alwyn Featherston, *Battle for Mortain.*

Pyle, Ernie, "The Great Attack," in *Reporting World War II,* Part II. New York, 1995.

Rosenblum, Walter, quoted by Donald L. Miller, *The Story of World War II.*

Scannell, Vernon, *Argument of Kings.* London, 1987.

Schrijvers, Peter, *The Crash of Ruin: American Combat Soldiers in Europe During World War II.* New York, 1998.

Sharpe, Mitchell, quoted by Paul Fussell, ed., *The Norton Book of Modern War.* New York, 1991.

Simpson, Louis, *Selected Prose.* New York, 1989.

Sorel, Nancy Caldwell, *The Women Who Wrote the War.* New York, 1999.

Spiller, Roger, "My Guns: A Memoir of the Second World War," *American Heritage,* Dec. 1991, pp. 45–51.

Steere, Edward, *The Graves Registration Service in WWII.* Washington, DC, 1951.

Stouffer, Samuel A., et al., *The American Soldier: Combat and Its Aftermath.* 2 vols. Princeton, NJ, 1949.

Sugerman, Tracy, *My War.* New York, 2000.

Terkel, Studs, *"The Good War."* New York, 1984.
Tonkin, John, quoted in Max Hastings, *Das Reich.* New York, 1982.
28th Roll On: The Story of the 28th Infantry Division. n.p., n.d.

United States Strategic Bombing Survey, Summary Report. Washington, DC, 1997.

von Luck, Hans, *Panzer Commander.* New York, 1989.
Vonnegut, Kurt, *Slaughterhouse-Five.* New York, 1969.

Warlimont, Walter, *Inside Hitler's Headquarters, 1939–45,* trans. R. H. Barry. Novato, CA, 1962.
Webster, David, quoted by Stephen Ambrose in *Band of Brothers.* New York, 1992.
Weigley, Russell F., *Eisenhower's Lieutenants: The Campaigns of France and Germany, 1944–1945.* Bloomington, IN, 1981.
West, Nigel, introduction to Roger Heskith, *Fortitude: The D-Day Deception Campaign.* Woodstock, NY, 2000.
Whiting, Charles, *The Battle of Hürtgen Forest.* New York, 1990.
———, *Death of a Division.* New York, 1981.
Willis, Donald J., *The Incredible Year.* Ames, IA, 1988.
Winston, Keith, *Letters of a World War II Combat Medic,* ed. Sarah Winston. Chapel Hill, NC, 1985.
Winters, Richard, quoted by Stephen Ambrose in *Citizen Soldiers.*
Wood, Edward W., Jr., *On Being Wounded.* Golden, CO, 1991.

Suggestions for Further Reading

The universal catastrophe that was the Second World War can be merely hinted at in this little book. For a necessary context readers might turn to excellent one-volume histories by Sir John Keegan and Sir Martin Gilbert. Keegan's *The Second World War* (New York, 1989) takes *world* seriously, and in addition to sophisticated analysis of ground warfare in Europe devotes attention to events in Russia and the Pacific as well as in the air and on the sea. One of his most trenchant observations is this: "The Second World War must engage our moral sense. Its destructiveness, its disruption of legal and social order, were on a scale so disordinate that it cannot be viewed as a war among other wars. . . . Above all, Hitler's institution of genocide demands a moral commitment."

That commitment Keegan feels everywhere, and Gilbert feels it even more in his *The Second World War: A Complete History* (New York, 1989). Gilbert is a master of military geography, creator of numerous political and military atlases, and the copious maps in his 866-page volume are drawn by him. But a more telling characteristic is his sensitivity to human suffering and his acute awareness of Keegan's "moral dimension." He seldom writes about a battle or even a small encounter between armed enemies without pausing to tot up the butcher's bill in killed and maimed. (It can be said that it is the absence of this moral dimension that makes so much other military history seem affected and bizarre, if not sometimes unwittingly cruel.)

Another excellent and extremely accessible "complete history" of the war is Donald L. Miller's *The Story of World War II* (New York, 2001), an extraordinary expanded version of historian Henry Steele Commager's original text of 1945, updated and amply larded with fascinating soldier testimony from the now-aging participants.

Among this fading group is Robert Kotlowitz, whose memoir *Before Their Time* (New York, 1997) I have made much of. The troops' memoirs in my listing of sources will be found rewarding, especially to readers interested in exploring the fact that what has been celebrated as the Greatest Generation included among the troops and their officers plenty of criminals, psychopaths, cowards, and dolts.

The astonishing boyishness of the troops remains a fascinating subject, as in John P. Irwin's *Another River, Another Town,* whose subtitle is designed less to astonish than to report: *A Teenage Tank Gunner Comes of Age in Combat—1945* (New York, 2002).

Access to unchanging infantry problems and actualities is provided by Keegan's *The Face of Battle* (New York, 1976), and perhaps even more vividly by Joanna Bourke's *An Intimate History of Killing: Face to Face Killing in Twentieth-Century Warfare* (London, 1999). Another British author, John Ellis, has written two bright and honest books about the business of the infantry, *The Sharp End: The Fighting Man in World War II* (London, 1990) and, taking a wider view of air and sea warfare as well, *Brute Force: Allied Strategy and Tactics in the Second World War* (New York, 1990), which, in addition to treating Allied operations in the Pacific and Southeast Asia, analyzes critically ground combat in Europe between the invasion and the end. One critic of that book has noted that it "crackles with irritation," which suggests that it damages numerous sentimentalities and exposes many merely patriotic certainties.

There are numerous books about the famous leaders of the war in Europe. Gilbert's experience as Churchill's official biographer adds authority to his one-volume abridgment of his multivolume work, *Churchill: A Life* (New York, 1991). Eisenhower is superbly dealt with by his grandson David, whose *Eisenhower: At War, 1943–1945* (New York, 1986) is not just knowledgeable but judicious and sensible. Carlo D'Este's *Eisenhower: A Soldier's Life* (New York, 2002) offers interesting material, if excessively detailed, on Ike's boyhood and peacetime army life, but the final third of this 848-page book delivers invaluable insights on Ike's problems and decisions (not all wonderful) during World War II, and becomes a refreshingly critical workout by an expert on tactics, logistics, and military possibilities. D'Este is first-rate on the quarrels between British and American staffs, which, it can be argued, delayed the end of the war many months and would have profoundly affected the morale and performance of the troops, had they but known.

Readers interested in the unpublicized and unbloody war for strategic superiority between the British and the Americans will be enlightened by Lord Alanbrooke's *War Diaries, 1939–1945*, edited by Alex Danchev and Daniel Todman (London, 2001), which can be countered by Martin Blumenson's edition of *The Patton Papers* (New York, 1972, 1974). Nigel Hamilton's *Monty: The Battles of Field Marshal Bernard Montgomery* (New York, 1994) does justice to his military knowledge as well as exhibiting his profoundly offensive personality.

Those interested in military history should explore the immense world of the multivolume official history *United States Army in World War II*, published in Washington, D.C., and finally finished in 1993. Like other works perpetrated by committees, it is sound but not very exciting (with the exception of Martin Blumenson's work). It can be supplemented by Russell F. Weigley's excellent *Eisenhower's Lieutenants: The Campaigns of France and Germany, 1944–1945* (Bloomington, IN, 1981). A more informal account of the American fighting in Europe is Charles B. MacDonald's *The Mighty Endeavor: American Armed Forces in the European Theater in World War II* (New York, 1969), which, in addition to covering events in North Africa, Sicily, and Italy, gives authoritative attention to much of the material I have dealt with. MacDonald's work is illuminated by his experience as a wartime company officer in the infantry. His *Company Commander* (Washington, 1947) was one of the first memoirs of the American ground war, and it is still solid and instructive.

A valuable book less about battle than social and political life at the time is William L. O'Neill's *A Democracy at War: America's Fight at Home and Abroad in World War II* (New York, 1993). O'Neill offers a fascinating survey of the special American world where national decisions, especially about mass-murderous enterprises, must be based on what the populace, which provides the cannon fodder, will understand and tolerate.

NOTE

Readers should realize that all writing sent from the front lines, like Keith Winston's letters or Ernie Pyle's press dispatches, had to pass rigorous censorship. To a soldier's homebound observations by V-mail or letter, the censorship was applied by one of his company officers wielding his little PASSED BY CENSOR rubber stamp, which, with stamp pad, he carried everywhere. The writing and pictures by official, accredited reporters and photographers had to pass censorship in Paris or New York. The result was that during the war, nothing really nasty as the troops knew it could reach nonmilitary minds, and readers of this book should realize that even when writers describe gruesome experiences and sights, the most appalling details have probably been excised or softened. Things were worse than they were allowed to seem, and many were literally unspeakable.

Index

About the Author

Paul Fussell was born in California and educated at Pomona College and Harvard. In the Second World War he was severely wounded in France as a twenty-year-old second lieutenant leading a rifle platoon in the 103rd Infantry Division. He has taught English at Connecticut College, Rutgers, the University of Heidelberg, King's College, London, and the University of Pennsylvania. He has received fellowships from the National Foundation for the Humanities and the Guggenheim and Rockefeller Foundations. His books include *The Great War and Modern Memory*, which won the National Book Award and the National Book Critics Circle Award; *Abroad: British Literary Traveling Between the Wars*; *Wartime: Understanding and Behavior in the Second World War*; and *Doing Battle: The Making of a Skeptic*. He is married to journalist Harriette Behringer and lives in Philadelphia.